Multi-Sensory Message

Ready-to-use Bible-based sessions on mission
– for creative churches, youth groups and small groups

Dave Maclure

INTERSERVE
. . . . england and wales

MULTI-SENSORY MESSAGE by Dave Maclure

Scripture Union, 207–209 Queensway, Bletchley, MK2 2EB, UK

email: info@scriptureunion.org.uk

www.scriptureunion.org.uk

Scripture Union Australia: Locked Bag 2, Central Coast Business Centre, NSW 2252

www.su.org.au

ISBN 978 1 84427 273 0

First published in Great Britain by Scripture Union 2008

© Dave Maclure

British Library Cataloguing-in-Publication data: a catalogue record for this book is available from the British Library.

Cover design by waldonwhitejones of Basildon, Essex, UK

Internal page design by Creative Pages: www.creativepages.co.uk

Printed and bound by Henry Ling Limited, at the Dorset Press, Dorchester, DT1 1HD

Scripture Union is an international Christian charity working with churches in more than 130 countries providing resources to bring the good news about Jesus Christ to children, young people and families – and to encourage them to develop spiritually through the Bible and prayer. As well as coordinating a network of volunteers, staff and associates who run holidays, church-based events and school Christian groups, Scripture Union produces a wide range of publications and supports those who use their resources through training programmes.

Contents

For

Rachel and Nelson,
and in loving memory of Krish Rockley.

Thanks

Thanks need to go out to many people who have helped towards the completion of this book. The ideas contained here stem from the creativity and passion I have witnessed in others in their communication of the Message.

So, in no particular order, I would like to express my gratitude to the World Mission Committee, the International Cell Group and the endlessly imaginative staff of St Michael le Belfrey; Friends International colleagues for their helpful input at conferences and training events; staff past and present of the Barbican Bookshop, York; the three Scripture Union staff who I have had direct contact with – editor Lin Ball, and former *Christis* buddies Peter Thomas and Matthew Campbell. Lastly, big thanks to Ruth Leckenby whose last-minute proofreading was much appreciated!

A special note of thanks to my dear folks and my extraordinary extended family for teaching me the beauty of the Message and its relevance for every living thing in the whole world.

This publication is a partnership project with INTERSERVE, who have provided the case study material of real mission stories from around the world.

INTERSERVE is an inter-denominational Christian missions agency with over 150 years experience of showing God's love in a practical and biblical way to the marginalised and unreached peoples of Asia, the Arab World, the UK and, more recently, mainland Europe. Its holistic approach to mission with its unique matching of professional people skills with their heart for the lost ensures that communities are served, relationships are built and gospel love is both shown and said.

With 19 sending offices and over 700 Partners scattered across more than 25 countries, including some of the most dangerous in the world, Interserve is well placed to share the love of Christ with the people its Partners meet. If you would like to know more about short or long term service with Interserve, call 01908 552700 or email enquiries@isewi.org

Making the most of Multi-Sensory Message

We all need to grow as Christians and studying the Bible is a vital part of that growth. However, all too often, Bible study can degenerate into dreariness or study groups slide into cosy social gatherings. The *Multi-Sensory* series is designed to breathe life and vitality into the process of maturing in Christ, as well as deepening fellowship and helping everyone move faith into action.

Multi-Sensory Message is aimed at helping creative groups in various settings explore what the Bible has to say about how the message of the gospel is communicated and sent into the world. This is a huge topic and so the sessions are wide-ranging rather than narrowly focused. The material is intended as a 'menu' from which you can select. For complete flexibility it is structured in nine complete sessions with options, followed by a number of stand-alone extra activities. Wherever possible we have provided photocopiable templates to give maximum support to those leading.

Reading the Bible

Remember that not everyone finds it easy to find their way around the Bible, so give people plenty of time to find passages and look up references. You will find it helpful to vary the way the Bible is read in the group or service, and think about using different Bible versions and ways of presenting the passage visually and aurally.

Using the material your way

If you want to focus on mission for a period of time in your church or small group you can work consecutively through all nine sessions, selecting the material that best suits you and adding in any of the additional activities towards the back of the book. If your timetable or church programme doesn't allow for nine sessions, be selective. Or you may wish to use the material to put on a week or weekend with special emphasis on mission, perhaps including an invitation to a guest speaker.

The sessions in **Multi-Sensory Message** are built around a common 'menu' approach:

 ## Getting connected (allow 10–15 minutes)

This icebreaker will get everyone involved and sharing together from the very beginning. It is easy to see the value of this part of a session when a group is just starting out or when new people have recently joined, but even if you have known each other for a long time you will often be surprised at what you discover.

 ## Touching God (allow 15–20 minutes)

Jesus encouraged his followers to engage with God through all their senses. For example:

Look at the birds of the air – Matthew 6:26.

My sheep **listen** to my voice – John 10:27.

Touch me and see – Luke 24:39.

Take and **eat**; this is my body – Matthew 26:26.

She has done a beautiful thing (when Mary poured sweet-**smelling** perfume over Jesus) – Mark 14:6.

So that's the emphasis of this part of the session.

 ## Living Scripture (allow 40–45 minutes)

The aim is to search the Scriptures, but also to allow the Scriptures to search us. 'All Scripture is

God-breathed and is useful for teaching, rebuking, correcting and training in righteousness' (2 Timothy 3:16). Take a few moments to pray that God will inspire your discussion before you consider the questions.

Reaching out (allow 15–20 minutes)

It is easy to skip over this part of the meeting, particularly if you have let an earlier section run on too long. A group that stops looking outwards will soon become stagnant. **Reaching out** often includes an idea for a social activity as a great way of drawing new people into the group. Even if you don't use this part of the session every time, be sure to plan it into your programme occasionally.

Digging deeper

This is the optional 'homework' part of the evening for anyone who wants to continue to think about the theme between the sessions. It's supported by photocopiable bookmarks for the leader to give out for people to take away. If you have time and resources, why not laminate them?

Preparing well

Each of the sessions in **Multi-Sensory Message** includes a choice of material. Look ahead and decide which of the suggestions are right for your group. Many of the ideas require advance preparation – sometimes needing to be done not just the night before but over a period of weeks. Have everything ready before people arrive so you can concentrate on making them welcome. Don't be afraid to use the material as a springboard for your own ideas – adding your own touches, mixing and matching activities to suit your group.

Sharing the leadership

Sharing out responsibility for different parts of the meeting will strengthen the group. Work towards a rota where different people lead different sections each time. Meet in various homes so that everyone has the opportunity to give hospitality. Appoint an assistant leader and let them run the meeting from time to time. After all, if the group becomes too big to fit into one home, your assistant can start a second group!

Being people-minded

Be people-minded rather than programme-driven. Being welcoming is important. Timing is also important; start promptly and don't overrun. If you go on too late, people might think twice about coming back next time. Be aware of the quieter members and draw them in with a simple but direct question sometimes, such as, 'Chris, what do you think?' But be sensitive. If someone doesn't turn up, get in touch before the next meeting. The aim is not to pressurise people, but to let them know they matter. Pray regularly – daily if possible – for the members of your group.

Finally

Many of the ideas in **Multi-Sensory Message** have been used effectively in all sorts of gatherings, large and small. You'll find most can be adapted for school assemblies, retreats, quiet days, camps, conferences, training events, student outreach, church services, prayer meetings, etc. Step out and experiment. Let your imagination fly!

1 Creation – the message of hope

Genesis 1:27–31; 3:8–24; 12:1–5

Why do we 'do' mission? Why do Christians feel they have a message for the world? The answers to those questions start right at the beginning of the Bible story, in Genesis. Genesis presents us with (at least) two compelling reasons for Christians to communicate the truth about God's work and character.

Firstly, as part of God's creation 'made in his image' we have been designed to live in relationship with our Creator, with each other and with the created order around us. More than this, Genesis reveals that as descendants of Adam we are to reflect God's image to the world and we have a mandate for the care of all that's entrusted to us.

Secondly, Genesis presents us with the reality of human sin. The fall – the breakdown of the relationship of man with God and with creation – led to a curse that began with Adam and Eve and resulted in all humanity living at a distance from God, under his judgement. And yet Genesis leaves us with the promise of a solution. This solution was fully revealed in the person and work of Jesus Christ. His death and resurrection reversed the curse of Genesis and made the way possible for a new creation. This is the fantastic message we proclaim as Christians!

 Getting connected

Creation guessing game
You will need: scrap paper; pens; a bowl or hat.

Give everyone a piece of paper and a pen. Ask them to write three things on the paper, without letting anyone else see what they are writing:

- the name of their favourite animal;

- the name of an animal about which they have a phobia or dislike;

- the name of a memorable place of natural beauty they have visited.

Collect the slips of paper, scrunch them up, put them in a bowl and shake them up. Pass the bowl around and ask each person to take a piece. Go around the group, reading the things written down, and together try to guess who wrote them.

OR

Which creature?
If you could be any creature – on land, in the air or in the sea – which would you be, and why?

 Touching God

Beginning and end
Sing or listen to a worship song focusing on God the Creator. Encourage everyone to respond physically – choosing to sit, kneel, lift their hands, or dance.

A good choice to listen to would be 'Beginning and end' by Eden's Bridge, a Celtic worship band. (Available on their CD: *The Best of Celtic Praise and Worship Vol 1*, Straightway SWD80836.) The lyrics are about God as Creator and Sustainer of life. Play the song twice; it's quite short but the lyrics are worth reflecting on.

Good choices for singing include:

- 'All creatures of our God and King' (*Mission Praise*, 7; *Songs of Fellowship*, 645)

- 'God is great, amazing!' (*Songs of Fellowship*, 730; *The Source*, 126)

- 'Great is your faithfulness' (*Hymns for today's church*, 260; *Mission Praise*, 200; *The Source*, 138)

OR

God's questions

The book of Job ends with God speaking, mainly in rhetorical questions, about his Lordship over creation. This wonderful passage of scripture opens our eyes to the splendour of God's power in making the world and everything in it. Stand and read Job 38:4–30 aloud, as dramatically as you can. Change reader every time you come to a question mark in the text. You could add to the atmosphere by playing some dramatic classical music in the background.

OR

Creation praise

Invite people to bring in a small object or creature from the natural world – a piece of moss, a snail, a dandelion, a pebble. Collect them on a tray in the centre of the group and use them as a centrepiece for a time of praise to God for the world he has created.

 Living Scripture – Genesis 1:27–31; 3:8–24; 12:1–5

1   Read Genesis 1:27–31. In the unspoiled creation, what role did Adam and Eve – and, by extension, all humanity – have in God's world?

2   Read Genesis 3:8–24. How are the relationships between God, people and the rest of creation distorted and damaged by the disobedience of Adam and Eve? What evidence do you see of humanity's separation from God in the world today?

3   This passage centres on the curse of the fall, but is there any indication of a solution?

4   Fast forward to Genesis 12:1–5 where we read of God's promise to Abraham. How has this promise come true? How is it still coming true?

 Reaching out

Blessings scroll

You will need: A4 photocopies of page 10, one for each person; pens; matches (optional); hot water; tea bags; paint brushes.

God's promise in Genesis 12 was that all peoples on earth would be blessed through Abraham's descendants. One of Abraham's descendants was Jesus, who made this blessing of God fully possible. This activity encourages us to rejoice and testify that God's promise to Abraham still holds true for us today.

In true *Blue Peter* fashion, it would be good to have tried out this activity in advance so that you have a finished scroll to show.

Under the printed heading write 'Abraham' – as the first to be blessed from this promise – followed by rows of dots down the page symbolising the billions of people who have since benefited from

God's blessing. About halfway down the page, people should write in the name of their church, then below that the names of some or all of the others in the group or congregation, and lastly their own name. Roll the sheet of paper at either end to make it curl like a scroll.

For even more authenticity, make the scroll look ancient and weather-worn. Gently rip the very edges of the paper and singe them carefully with a match. Take great care that adults perform this part of the activity on behalf of any children in the group. It's also a good idea to have a bowl of water to hand just in case someone is over enthusiastic! Then, soak the tea bags in hot water and use brushes to paint this solution over the scroll. The finished item should look something like this.

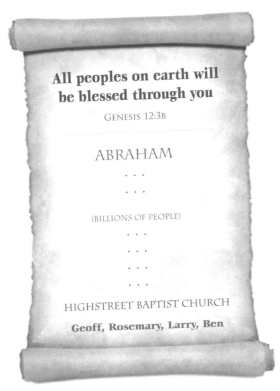

Explain that the scroll represents the ongoing generations of all those who have benefited from the promise of God to Abraham in Genesis 12. Spend some time thanking God for his amazing promises that bless us today, so many years after they were given. Thank God for the fulfilment of the promise in Jesus. Then pray for those you know – friends and family – whose names you long to see included on the list. Take the scrolls home as a reminder of God's promise.

OR

Case study 1: A better understanding
Have a good reader read Case study 1 from page 51, about an Interserve staff worker with the Christian environmental organisation, A Rocha. Where there is a break in the text, pause the reading to discuss: What do you think happened? What would you have done if you were the A Rocha staff worker?

Spend some time praying for the work of A Rocha and other Christian people or organisations you know who are involved in environmental work.

If you have time, brainstorm ideas of how you can live in a way that reflects a desire to care for creation. Choose one new idea each to try and implement (such as recycling more, switching off TVs at the socket instead of leaving them on standby etc). At your next session, report honestly how you got on.

 Digging deeper

Give each person a copy of the bookmark on page 56 to take home, with encouragement to use it during the coming week.

GOD'S PROMISE

All peoples on earth will be blessed through you

GENESIS 12:3B

2 The message of blessing

Psalm 67

The purpose and end of mission is worship and joy for all people. Mission rests on God's promise to save all the people of the world; to rescue them from the judgement they deserve; and to make them a nation of his own. Because of this, the people of God should be characterised by joyful praise as they live out and communicate this message. Revelation 7 paints a picture of worship before the throne of God as multitudes assemble in eternal praise. Psalm 67, only seven verses long and without a known author, provides a rich vision of this life of worship lived now, both in the light of past promises and in the hope of future blessings.

For the Israelites in the Old Testament, this psalm was a reminder of two important things. Firstly, God's promise of blessing as given to Abraham was still being worked out; a day of abundant blessing lay ahead. Secondly, the blessings they had received from God were to be mirrored in the world for the benefit of all people. The party was to be for everybody – not just the direct descendants of Abraham.

 ## Getting connected

Blessings shared

You will need: scrap paper; pens.

Think of a time God blessed you in an unexpected way. Spend five minutes writing an account, as concisely as you can. Read your stories to each other or in pairs.

OR

Harvest memories

Has anyone in the group lived or worked on a farm? In advance, prepare one or two people to talk about their memories of harvest.

 ## Living Scripture – Psalm 67

Begin this exploration of the psalm with a short meditation.

You will need: photocopies of pages 14, 15 and 16 for everyone; quiet background music (optional). Alternatively, if you have access to a multimedia projector and a laptop you could project images evoked by the psalm onto a wall, such as a shining sun, a straight road leading to the horizon, athletes carrying flags into the Olympic Games, people worshipping, harvest fields, the world seen from space.

Ask your designated reader to read the psalm aloud slowly, pausing between each verse, while the rest of the group look at the images.

After the reading, pray briefly that God will make his ways known through his Word. Then discuss the questions.

1   What is the connection between verse 1 and verse 2? How will God's ways be known on earth and his salvation to all nations?

2   Verses 2–5 are directed toward God in adoration. What aspects of God's character does the psalmist remind us about? Do you see any evidence of God demonstrating these attributes in our day?

3. The psalm concludes as it began, with an appeal for God to bless us and for his glory to extend into the world. In what ways would you like to see this happen in your life; in the lives of the people you know; in the wider world?

 Touching God

Psalm 67 remixed

Invite everyone, either working singly or in pairs, to write a version of Psalm 67 in their own words. The style can be informal or formal, rhyming or not rhyming, poetic, contemporary – anything! The psalm is for 'stringed instruments' so if you play guitar (or another stringed instrument) you could write something to set to music. If you're feeling brave, polish your efforts and ask your church leaders about sharing them in church!

Here are two different examples to read to give people some inspiration!

Psalm 67 remixed

God, be good to us!

Send us your best vibes, big hugs and wide smiles.

God, I want this so people can see you more clearly –
 in Tenerife, Greenland, Cricklewood, Istanbul, Las Vegas,
 Nairobi, Argentina… you name it…
 let's see your salvation everywhere!
Let's have everyone praising you, God,
 from the rooftops nice and loud;
 huge crowds of people singing lung-busting anthems to you, God!
I want this because your steady hand is behind everything,
 guiding the nations according to your plans.

Then we will see proper solutions and real peace for everybody,
 for the lowly or the loaded,
 the sick or the sound,
 the victims or the villains,
 the overworked or the out of work,
 the influential or the invisible.
And so let's have everyone respecting our awesome God!

Psalm 67 remixed

May God be gracious to us and bless us.
May his face shine on us from above,
To touch us, to heal us and to caress us.

May God's ways be known upon the earth,
The sphere of the globe, the land and the sea:
Giving salvation, new life of infinite worth.

May all peoples sing a joyful refrain
To you, our righteous guide and ruler
And may all the nations find joy in your name.

Then our land a bountiful harvest will yield
And God will bless us, his face shine on us,
And the world will fear our protector, our shield.

OR

Harvest grain

You will need: a small sack (or cloth bag) of grain or corn kernels.

Open the sack in front of the group and let it spill out. Pick up a handful of grain and slowly let it filter through your fingers. As you do so, pray for a blessing and unexpected harvest in your life, in the lives of the people you know and in the wider world. Invite the group to take it in turns to do the same. Following each prayer, you could say Psalm 67:7 together as a group:

God will bless us, and all the ends of the earth will fear him.

Reaching out

Famine relief

Using data researched in advance, pray about one area of the world currently suffering harvest failure, drought or famine. Could your group take part in a sponsored fast or organise an event to raise money for a charity that is doing relief work in that part of the world?

Digging deeper

Give each person a copy of the bookmark on page 56 to take home, with encouragement to use it during the coming week.

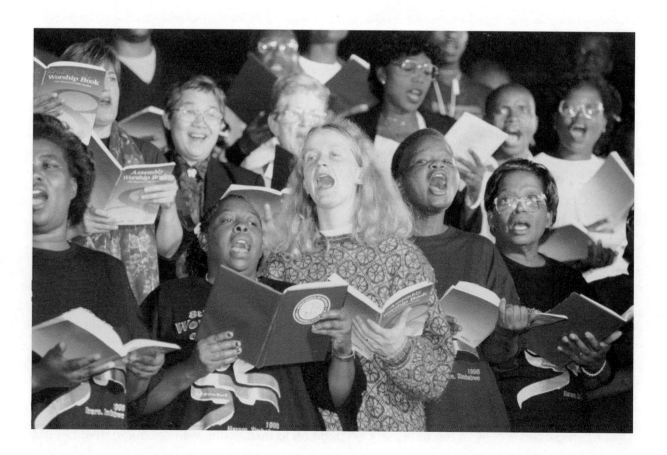

3 The message for the least deserving

Jonah

Is there somebody you find hard to get along with? Does the prospect of having a conversation with them sap your energy and fill you with dread? Maybe this is how Jonah felt when asked to speak to the Ninevites – a brutal group of people with a reputation for violence. It's easy to understand why Jonah might have been daunted by God's command for him to go and preach his message to them.

We all love the tale of Jonah, especially the bit where he gets swallowed by a big fish! And yet, this mysterious book tucked in among the pages of the minor prophets is much more than a children's story. Jonah's four short chapters contain a complex dialogue between God, his prophet and a people in need of salvation.

The book of Jonah shows us we have a God concerned about the people who seemed to be the least deserving of his mercy. It also shows us that – in spite of our own foibles, doubts, frailty and even disobedience – God can use us, just as he did Jonah.

Note: Some more activities on the book of Jonah can be found in *Multi-Sensory Together*, pages 27–31.

 Getting connected

What a day I've had!
Photocopy page 20 and cut into strips. Randomly distribute the slips among the group. Tell them to read theirs without divulging to others what it says. Explain that they have to say the phrase, 'What a day I've had!' in the style of the adjective or phrase on their slip of paper. In turn, everyone stands up and greets the others using only this phrase. Try to guess what each other's slip of paper has written on it. Finish by asking these two questions:

*   What sort of a day have you really had?

*   How would Jonah say 'What a day I've had!' after he had been thrown overboard and swallowed by a fish?

OR

Cruisin' around
Have you ever travelled a long distance by ship? Describe your experiences.

 Touching God

Animated Jonah
Watch the first few scenes of the DVD *Testament – the Bible in Animation: Jonah* (1998), up to the point where Jonah gets onto a boat headed in the wrong direction. How is the way God speaks to Jonah portrayed? What new insights do you gain from seeing the story creatively illustrated in this way?

OR

Dramatic Jonah

In pairs recreate God's call to Jonah (Jonah 1:2) in a contemporary setting. Decide how God might speak to Jonah today. What 'undeserving' people might he call Jonah to go to? And how might Jonah reply? After time for discussion, each pair can 'act out' the calling to the rest of the group.

 ## Living Scripture – Jonah

Read all of Jonah as if it were a play. *The Message* version of the Bible is good to use for this. You can access the Message online at www.biblegateway.com. You will need five people to take parts in the story: the narrator, Jonah, one person to represent the sailors, God, the King of Nineveh. After each chapter, pause and discuss briefly these same three questions:

1 What do you find surprising about the reactions of the people you just read about?

2 What aspects of the narrative did you find funny, serious, expected or unexpected?

3 Imagine you are hearing the story for the first time. What do you think is going to happen next?

After reading through the book discuss these questions:

4 The Ninevites were known for being a brutal people; culturally, religiously and ethically they were opposed to the Israelite way of life. How understandable is Jonah's response to God's call?

5 What places in the world might be 'our Nineveh' today? What would your reaction be if you felt God calling you to speak of him in those places? And how would you estimate your chances of getting those people to change?

6 Look again at 3:7–10 and 4:1–3. What do we learn about the attributes of God from these verses? Do you feel any differently now about your discussion of question 5?

 ## Reaching out

Should I not be concerned?

You will need: a selection of the day's newspapers.

The story of Jonah finishes abruptly with a question from God: 'Should I not be concerned about that great city?' This statement may have been difficult for the Israelites to hear. They considered themselves God's chosen people. Why should God care about the Ninevites: a group of violent, pagan, foreigners?

Sometimes we too are guilty of not being concerned for others in our world. Spend some time in quiet, reflecting on God's care for all people and all of creation. Then share out pages from the day's newspapers and, after a few minutes' reading, encourage everyone to offer one short prayer for any needy people they have read about. After each prayer, say together as a group: 'Lord, give me a concerned heart.'

OR

Case study 2: Woman to woman

Jonah had to travel a long distance to find the people God had called him to, a people very different from himself. And yet in our society today people from all over the world – with vastly different experiences from ourselves – live in our own cities and towns. Give out photocopies of Case study 2 from page 52, a true and dramatic story of Interserve mission work in the UK. Ask the group to read it silently.

Let the story lead you into a time of prayer. Pray that the many people of other faiths and cultures living on our doorsteps will come to the living water and satisfy their thirst. Pray that God will give wisdom and boldness to Christians who are reaching out to people like Fatma. Pray that others will catch the vision and make the most of opportunities God has given us.

OR

Prayer walk
Go for a 10–15 minute walk around your immediate neighbourhood, thinking and praying about the 'least deserving' in the community. Come together at the end to share any thoughts God may have given you for an outreach initiative.

Note: If you have time at the end of the evening, why not finish watching the animation film?

 Digging deeper

Give each person a copy of the bookmark on page 56 to take home, with encouragement to use it during the coming week.

What a day I've had!

Angry
Late for an appointment
Tired
Sad
Your team have just won the final!
Secretive
Startled
Upset, tearful
You're in love!
Feeling ill
Confused

4 The message in person – Jesus!

Luke 2:21–40

He is given the name Emmanuel – 'God with us'. Jesus is born! The author and finisher of the message arrives! The solution for the Eden curse is bound up in the life, ministry, death and resurrection of Jesus of Nazareth. The judgement we deserve as sinful humanity is reversed for those who believe in him. New life, restored relationships with God, each other and our creation begin at the empty tomb. This good news is the message we proclaim!

After the birth of Jesus, he is presented at the temple by Joseph and Mary in accordance with Israelite law. There they encounter two people. The words of Simeon and Anna in Luke 2 offer an insight into who this baby would become. I wonder what Mary and Joseph thought as the implications sank in concerning the young life in their care. Bystanders watching this scene may have been both confused and exhilarated. This Galilean baby is God's salvation? And he is here today?

Note: If you choose the **Getting connected** activity **Helping us on our way**, you will need to invite the group in advance to bring in pictures of themselves as babies.

 ## Getting connected

Role models
Discuss: how have other Christians influenced you in your faith?

OR

Helping us on our way
Using their own baby pictures as visual aids, ask each person to describe the people who were essential in their life when they were babies.

 ## Living Scripture – Luke 2:21–40

Read the passage as a group, each person reading a paragraph.

1 Simeon's prayer reads like a prophecy. What was his vision for the life of Jesus?

2 Simeon's words to Mary in verses 34 and 35 are cryptic and loaded with imagery. What do you think they mean in light of the life Jesus lived?

3 What is your impression of Anna from the fleeting three-verse description of her life?

4 What might Mary and Joseph have thought concerning what was said about Jesus?

5 How does this passage increase your vision for who Jesus is?

 ## Touching God

Mini-biography
You will need: pens; paper; coloured felt-tip pens; gentle classical music to play in the background (optional).

Luke 2 describes for us, in an abridged format, the lives of two godly older people – Simeon and Anna. How would you like your life to be remembered? Write a 60-word biography or draw a pictorial representation of what you would want people to say about you and your faith when you approach the end of your life. In pairs, share your biographies. Reflect on your life now. In what ways do you need to change to reach the ideal you wrote about or drew? Pray for each other, for the Spirit to mould you into the likeness of Jesus.

OR

Proclaim the coming King

This proclaiming activity is more suitable for larger groups or a whole congregation.

Photocopy the page opposite and distribute so that everybody can see a copy. Read it together, following the directions included, letting your posture symbolise a joyful progression towards praise.

You may want to invite individuals to respond with short spontaneous prayers of thanks following the reading.

 Reaching out

Words of wisdom

Plan to invite an older Christian to come to your group to talk about how they have maintained their enthusiasm for communicating their faith over the years. Or invite a retired missionary or church leader to come and talk about their experiences of communicating the message during their time of active ministry. [Interserve is always happy to supply speakers for groups; see the contact details on page 4.]

OR

Words of appreciation

Write a letter of thanks to an older person who helped you to understand about Jesus; or a letter of encouragement to a missionary you have met.

 Digging deeper

Give each person a copy of the bookmark on page 57 to take home, with encouragement to use it during the coming week.

Proclaim the coming King

Psalm 145 for group reading

Leader *(seated)*

I will exalt you, my God the King;
     I will praise your name for ever and ever.
Every day I will praise you
     and extol your name for ever and ever.

Men only *(seated)*

Great is the LORD and most worthy of praise;
     his greatness no one can fathom.
One generation will commend your works to another;
     they will tell of your mighty acts.
They will speak of the glorious splendour of your majesty,
     and I will meditate on your wonderful works.
They will tell of the power of your awesome works,
     and I will proclaim your great deeds.
They will celebrate your abundant goodness
     and joyfully sing of your righteousness.

Women only *(seated)*

The LORD is gracious and compassionate,
     slow to anger and rich in love.
The LORD is good to all;
     he has compassion on all he has made.
All you have made will praise you, O LORD;
     your saints will extol you.
They will tell of the glory of your kingdom
     and speak of your might,
so that all men may know of your mighty acts
     and the glorious splendour of your kingdom.

Leader *(who now stands)*

Your kingdom is an everlasting kingdom,
     and your dominion endures through all generations.

Men *(standing now)*

The LORD is faithful to all his promises
     and loving toward all he has made.
The LORD upholds all those who fall
     and lifts up all who are bowed down.

Women *(standing now)*

The eyes of all look to you,
     and you give them their food at the proper time.
You open your hand
     and satisfy the desires of every living thing.

Everyone together *(standing, arms outstretched in praise)*

The LORD is righteous in all his ways
     and loving toward all he has made.
The LORD is near to all who call on him,
     to all who call on him in truth.
He fulfils the desires of those who fear him;
     he hears their cry and saves them.
The LORD watches over all who love him,
     but all the wicked he will destroy.

Everyone together
(shouting loudly)

My mouth will speak in praise of the LORD.
     Let every creature praise his holy name
     for ever and ever.

5 Training manual for messengers

Matthew 10

Jesus gave clear instructions to his disciples before they embarked on mission within Israel and we are very privileged to have these instructions recorded for us in Matthew 10. It's a challenging passage of scripture which reads like a training manual for extreme discipleship! Jesus emphasises:

- the proclamation of the good news

- unbridled generosity

- the centrality of prayer for healing and deliverance

- risky living by faith.

These factors have formed the basis for mission work in the Church for centuries.

This session focuses on the reality of suffering in the life of any Christian who seeks to promote their faith. As your group works through the study, encourage everyone to consider how the verses apply to their own lives and mission in this country. In the **Reaching out** section there is a chance for the group to explore some of the serious challenges facing the worldwide Church in our day – all in the context of remembering that God promises to sustain us, care for us and give us the strength (and even give the words to say) – when we carry out kingdom work.

 ## Getting connected

Only the essentials

If you could take only a carrier bag for your things when going on a long journey, what essential items would you put in it?

OR

Persecution and joy

William Barclay once said that disciples of Christ can expect two things: that they will be persecuted; but also that they will experience immense joy. Discuss briefly in pairs to what extent you think this is a fair summary of what it means to be a follower of Jesus.

 ## Touching God

Quiet reflection

Matthew 10 contains some strong and startling words of Jesus. Encourage your group to prepare themselves to be challenged! Begin by inviting them to spend ten minutes in silence. The aim of this time is to come gently into God's presence in preparation for studying his Word. Make full use of whatever space you have available. If you are meeting in a house (and with the host's permission!), suggest that some of the group move to other rooms (or even outside in the garden if that's practical) to avoid distracting each other. Before they go, lead them in this short prayer:

> *Dear Lord,*
> *lift the burdens from our shoulders;*
> *still the thoughts of our minds;*

wash away the sin from our hearts.
Remind us of your character;
focus our minds on your Word;
show us the truths we need to learn;
strengthen us to live our lives for you,
in your name.
Amen.

OR

Living like doves

Take time to look at some images of doves. There are many portrayals of the dove of peace available in art reference books from your local library or via the Internet. Also look at some pictures of real doves – again available from reference books on birds, or available on such websites as www.gotpetonline.com.

After looking at a selection, discuss why you think Jesus sent out his disciples with advice to be 'innocent as doves'. What might that mean, practically, in today's world?

 ## Living Scripture – Matthew 10

You will need: a flipchart for Question 5 (optional).

Read the passage together. It's quite a long chapter, so share the reading between the group members.

1   Look at Matthew 10:7,8. Sometimes mission work is seen simply as 'preaching the good news'. What do these two verses tell us about 'the complete package' of things a disciple of Christ can expect to do? What experience do you have of these different aspects?

2   Focus on Matthew 10:9,10. For some Christians, a minimalist lifestyle goes hand in hand with effective mission and radical discipleship. Other Christians consider it important to live materially as others do so as to have a platform of common interests from which to share the gospel. Discuss these views and their application to us today in the light of these verses.

3   In pairs, skim-read the rest of Chapter 10. What are some of the costs that disciples of Christ can expect to pay? Pick out some examples to discuss with the wider group.

4   What is your reaction to the kinds of things Jesus expected would happen to the disciples?

5   Now, look more closely at Matthew 10:19,20,26,29–31. List the promises and assurances we are given as we follow Jesus. How do they add to what has already been discussed?

The central theme of the passage is summed up in 10:38,39: '... and anyone who does not take up his cross and follow me is not worthy of me. Whoever finds his life will lose it, and whoever loses his life for my sake will find it.' Meditate on these words in silence for a few minutes and then pray together as a group over the things you have learned from the passage.

 ## Reaching out

Me, involved in mission?

You will need: an egg timer (optional).

Remind the group that mission is not just about 'over there' but is also about growing God's kingdom locally. Has anyone in the group ever been involved in mission – short term or longer term; in your own community; cross-cultural; overseas? Share your experiences briefly, describing one 'high' and one 'low' point of the time. If there are several contributors and you want to limit the time spent on this, challenge each person to speak only as long as the egg timer sand lasts!

Then ask those who have not been involved in mission if they would consider going. Encourage them to share their thoughts and concerns.

Pray for opportunities for everybody to be involved in using their gifts in taking the message out – at work or school, at home, or on a planned mission.

Think radically. Could you consider doing planned mission together as a group? If there is any enthusiasm from the group, talk to your leaders about the opportunities available locally or abroad.

short term mission, **long term impact**

On Track is Interserve's short term overseas programme which invites men and women from the ages of 18-70 to serve overseas in a capacity which matches their skills. Whether you want to go for two months or two years, **On Track** has hundreds of opportunities, ranging from Bible teachers to home-school teachers, designers, bakers, doctors, editors, vets, medics and so on. Many young people use **On Track** to explore God's call on their lives, and all are guaranteed life-changing experiences. If you would like to know more you can contact jenny@isewi.org.

What should you do if you sense that your group lacks any real enthusiasm for mission? You could turn this activity into a discussion, inviting people first to give honest opinions about their disinterest or fears related to mission. Challenge them to consider why mission work is relevant. Think about the biblical mandate and the outcomes of apathy of a Church disengaged with people's needs, and then go on to discuss local concerns that are perhaps more visible and immediate than those of other countries.

OR

Case study 3: The human face of HIV
Jesus' command to his disciples in Matthew 10:8 says, 'Heal the sick, raise the dead, cleanse those who have leprosy, drive out demons. Freely you have received, freely give.' In our day, AIDS is a catastrophic disaster that affects nearly 40 million people across the world. Like leprosy in Jesus' day, HIV sufferers are often treated as pariahs in their societies. Ask your group these questions for discussion:

1   What do you know about AIDS and its health and social effects?

2   How should we as Christians live out Matthew 10:8 in view of the AIDS pandemic?

Give out photocopies of the Interserve case study on page 53, which describes a true story of one way Christians are seeking to meet the desperate needs of those affected by AIDS. You could take turns to read a paragraph each.

3   Did you learn anything new from this story about how AIDS affects people's lives?

4   How do you feel, hearing a story like this?

Pray for Christians involved in ministering to those affected by HIV – including Christian doctors in your own country. Pray that many like Kavita may find the peace that passes all understanding, and an eternal hope in Jesus Christ.

OR

The suffering Church

Jesus' words in Matthew 10 make clear that his disciples will experience suffering because of their faith. Use this activity to explore this challenge.

Photocopy pages 28 and 29 and cut out the scenario slips. You may want to research more information about persecuted Christians to aid the prayer time at the end. Two good organisations are The Barnabas Fund (www.barnabasfund.org/) and Voice of the Martyrs (www.persecution.com).

Divide your group into pairs and give one scenario to each pair. Give the groups five minutes to read, discuss and come up with some answers for the question, 'What should I do?' The pairs should then feed back their ideas to the whole group. If you have time, continue discussion with these questions:

1   Do you think you could personally live out the advice you have suggested?

2   In your opinion, which person is in the most challenging situation?

Each of these scenarios is based on the experiences of real people. Close by spending some time praying for Christians around the world who face difficult decisions on a daily basis.

OR

Play the **Mission Impossible** board game (see pages 40, 41 and 60).

 Digging deeper

Give each person a copy of the bookmark on page 57 to take home, with encouragement to use it during the coming week.

The suffering Church

Marcus

Hi, I'm Marcus. In my country, people are very suspicious of the church I attend. Things were not so bad in the past, but a new political leader has begun to incite people against us. Three months ago we were told to leave our church building and all our chairs were taken away. We now meet in the pastor's home. Every day I hear on the news about more laws restricting what Christians can and cannot do. Inside I feel tense – part of me wants to hide, another part of me wants to fight. And yet another part of me wants to give up my faith altogether, as life would be so much easier. What should I do?

Angela

My name's Angela and I'm an international student. Praise God, I recently became a Christian here in the UK! I am just finishing my course and will soon return home to Taiwan. I am looking forward to seeing my boyfriend for the first time in two years and my parents too. The thing is, I know they won't be pleased about my new faith as they are Buddhists. I'm not sure if there's even a church for me to attend when I get home. I am enthusiastic to share my new faith but I am scared of the consequences if I speak too much about it when I return. What should I do?

Frank

Hello, I'm Frank and I work in a company in a wealthy, industrialised country. Sometimes I'm frustrated by things that happen at work. My boss has a very anti-Christian outlook and is often hostile to me. For example, when my department used pirated computer software I refused to install it on my machine, so my boss threatened to sack me. I don't want to lose my job and get a bad reference. And another thing – the company policy is that I can't even celebrate Easter and Christmas publicly. Any cards or decorations that are religious are banned! I get on with my colleagues OK and even try to tell them about my faith sometimes, but they rarely listen to me. What should I do?

Ahmed

I became a Christian through a dream in which Jesus appeared to me. My name is Ahmed and I am from a country where it is illegal to convert to Christianity. I have learned about the Bible from a website on the Internet. I am unsure what to do; professing my faith will lead to imprisonment or execution. If I flee I will never see my family again and I will bring shame to my father. I could continue with life as normal if I keep my new faith a secret. I have never met another Christian personally. What should I do?

Li

I am a Korean pastor and my name is Li. I have just been imprisoned and I am frequently tortured and beaten. What is my crime? Trying to smuggle Bibles into a Communist country. I may be released at any time – but it may not be for 10 or 20 years, possibly never. I have a young family and I am desperate to be with my wife, and to see my young children grow up. The guards tell me that if I sign a paper saying 'There is no God' I will be released today. What should I do?

Amy

Hey, I'm Amy, 15 years old and I live in the UK. I am occasionally bullied at school because of my weight problem. My dad is a vicar and I'm the only Christian in my year. I know I should say more about my faith, but by talking about Jesus I might draw attention to myself and create more excuses for others to pick on me. So, most of the time I stay very quiet and don't even tell people I go to church. Sometimes I prefer to tell people my dad is a lawyer as it just makes my life a bit easier if people don't think my family is weird because we are religious. What should I do?

Maria

My name is Maria and I live in a part of the world caught up in war. My husband has a Christian bookshop in the city, but recently the shop was burned down at night. So right now we have little income. As Christians we are caught in the middle: we are targets for our nation's enemies and our own people despise us. I am worried for the safety of our children and I think we should flee to my father's house in the countryside. My husband says this will not be any safer and, besides, we are in a better position than many people. He says we should stay to help those who are worse off. What should I do?

6 The Great Commission – getting the message out!

Matthew 28:16–20

The Great Commission is probably the most famous statement about Christian mission in the Bible, and has been especially important in the recent history of American and European mission. At just 50 words long (in the original Greek) these words have sparked waves of mission endeavour across the globe. Coming right at the end of Matthew, after Jesus' resurrection, they are taken by many Christians to be the last words and promise of Jesus before he ascended into heaven.

Getting connected

Confusing commission

The aim of the sketch (script on pages 74–77) is to introduce the topic of commissions. Use it to draw out the comical contrast between the Great Commission – unambiguous and authoritative – or Pierre de Brush's commission, which is shifting and vague.

Use these questions to help draw out the differences:

1   What were the terms of Pierre's commission? Did they stay the same?

2   What were the king's reasons for commissioning a painting?

3   What was the price of Pierre de Brush's commission?

Depending on the time available, you could simply read the sketch or give people a few props and a short time to read through before acting it out. This sketch could also be used in a service on the topic of the Great Commission.

OR

Personal experience

What is a commission? Have you ever been commissioned to do anything? Tell the group about it. How clearly was it described to you?

Living Scripture – Matthew 26:16–20

Read the passage together as a group.

1   Look at the reaction (verses 16,17) of the disciples to seeing the risen Jesus. How would you describe it?

2   The Great Commission includes a statement and a promise about Jesus (verses 18 and 20). Take some time to look at the phrasing of these truths. Are they clear? What do they cover? How are they an encouragement to Christians about to begin mission work?

3   Verse 19 begins, 'Therefore'. Why?

4   The commission itself is to Jesus' followers and, by extension, includes us today. It says we are to 'go and make disciples of all nations'. What is a disciple? Why are baptism and teaching singled out as central?

5   How daunting a task do you think the Great Commission would have sounded to the first disciples? Thinking about the support available then and now, is it more or less daunting for us today?

6   How relevant is the Great Commission to us today? How does it relate to us in our families, work, church and the wider world?

 Touching God

Post-it prayer

You will need: two large sheets of paper or card or two flip charts; a stack of Post-it notes. Write 'The authority of Jesus' in the middle of one sheet. Write 'The presence of Jesus' in the middle of the other one. Pin or Blu-tack these posters to a wall.

Distribute the Post-it notes so that each person in the group has two or three. Ask them to spend a few minutes reflecting on the authority and the presence of Jesus. Then they should write or draw anything that comes to mind about these two topics onto the notes and stick them on the posters. Standing around the posters, use the combined reflections of everyone as prompts for short prayers of thanks and praise.

OR

Inspirational poster

You will need: photocopies of the panel on page 32; a selection of pens, pencils and coloured felt-tip pens; sheets of A4 card.

Have a look at these three quotations from pioneering missionary to China, Hudson Taylor. Choose one of them to make into a poster which you can either take home and pin up as a challenge to yourself or give as a gift to someone else.

 Reaching out

Great Commission Burgers

You will need: photocopies of the Great Commission Burger from page 33, cut out, one for each person; coloured felt-tip pens.

Explain that the filling of the burger refers to our task as Jesus' disciples, but we are surrounded by the assurance of Jesus' ultimate authority and presence – the burger bun!

Into the top part of the bun everyone should write:

All authority in heaven and on earth has been given to me. Therefore:

In the 'filling' everyone should write:

Go and make disciples of all nations,
baptising them in the name of the Father and of the Son and of the Holy Spirit,
and teaching them to obey everything I have commanded you.

And in the other part of the bun everyone should write:

And surely I am with you always, to the very end of the age.

Matthew 28:18–20

Encourage them to put the burger on their fridge door or keep it in their wallet as a reminder of the Great Commission. You could also set the group the task of memorising the verses by the time you next have a meeting. Or, you could suggest that every time the group see their Great Commission Burgers, it could serve as a reminder to pray for a particular mission partner or project they know about.

OR

Case study 4: Should I stay or should I go?
Hand out photocopies of the Interserve Case study 4 from page 54 and read it aloud as an interview between two people. Discuss how people can know if God is calling them to overseas mission and pray for any professionals known to the group who have responded to such a call.

 Digging deeper

Give each person a copy of the bookmark on page 57 to take home, with encouragement to use it during the coming week.

Inspirational poster

'The Great Commission is not an option to be considered; it is a command to be obeyed.'

'God's work done in God's way will never lack God's supply.'

'God isn't looking for people of great faith, but for individuals ready to follow him.'

Hudson Taylor

The Great Commission Burger

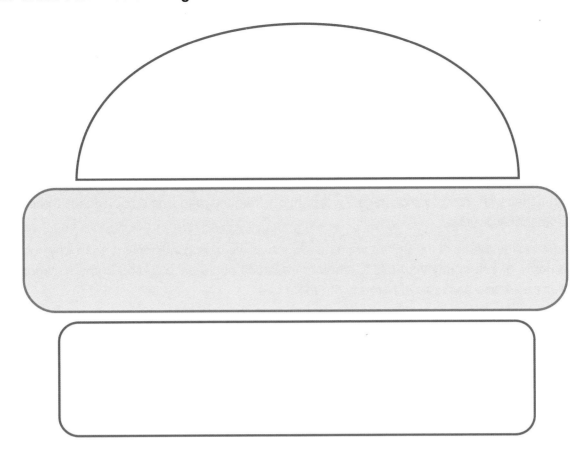

The Spirit comes with fire

7 Power to communicate the message

Acts 2

As Jesus ascended to heaven he promised he would send another counsellor – his Holy Spirit. The scared disciples huddled in Jerusalem waiting for the help to come. Nobody could have expected the events of Acts 2: wind, fire, the birth of the Church and a multitude of changed lives!

This session picks up on one theme in the passage in Acts in which all that is described – the theme of language and communication. In particular, attention is paid to the transformed Peter who preaches with clarity and courage – a distant cry from the man who denied Jesus three times in the Gospel accounts.

To underline the theme of the Spirit's fire (and as long as weather conditions permit!) why not meet in the home of somebody who has a real log fire which could be crackling in the background? Candles could also be displayed around the room.

Note: Another study of Acts 2 which emphasises different aspects of the account of Pentecost can be found in *Multi-Sensory Seasons*, pages 47–50.

 Getting connected

The Easiest Quiz
Photocopy **The Easiest Quiz** sheet from page 38, cutting along the lines as indicated and distributing so that there are enough for one per pair in your group. After you have divided your group into pairs (Player 1 and Player 2), give one half of the sheet to each person in the pair. Inform the group that this is The Easiest Quiz because answers will be given as you go along! Explain that everyone should read the instructions carefully and not show their quiz sheet to their partners until both players have finished.

When everyone has finished, ask them to compare their sheets. Are the answers they wrote down the same as those given? Why not? You can conclude the activity by agreeing that communication is not as easy as it seems – even when we speak the same language.

OR

Second language
Does anybody in the group speak a different language? Briefly describe your experiences of learning and using a new language.

OR

Communication mishaps
Can anybody think of any funny stories of miscommunication? Share them with the group.

 Living Scripture – Acts 2

This part of the session also refers to scriptures from Mark's Gospel: 8:29–33; 9:2–5 and 14:27–31. Ask three people to look these verses up beforehand and mark them, ready to read at the right time.

Read Acts 2 together as a group before tackling the questions.

1 How might the events of Acts 2 be described if they were being covered by a news broadcaster today?

2 Ask your three readers to read the Mark verses. What impression do you get of Peter from these readings? How does this compare with the Peter of Acts 2?

3 What is the climax of Peter's speech? Where does he draw his evidence from to support his argument?

4 Look at verses 41–47. What characterised the community of believers in Acts 2? What impression would it give if this happened in your town today?

 Touching God

The Spirit comes with fire
You will need: photocopies of the flame outline from page 33, printed onto sheets of yellow, orange and red paper or card and cut out, enough for three or four each; pens; Blu-tack; gentle music and candles to create a good ambiance (optional).

Acts 2 describes a time when the glory of God touched the disciples in a real and dramatic way with the coming of the Holy Spirit. And, with the power they received, they had incredible boldness in their outreach. In this activity you will spend time praying for the Holy Spirit to come down and make himself known to the group, giving them the courage to communicate the message. Therefore, this **Touching God** activity is also an alternative **Reaching out** activity.

Be sure to give a full explanation of this activity to the group. In particular, don't forget to mention that what they write on their sheets will be displayed for the group to see. Be aware that, for some Christians, spending time together praying for the Holy Spirit may be a new or unusual experience. Pray about this time before your meeting and talk to anybody in the group who you think may be uncomfortable with what happens. Ask your church leaders for advice if you feel you need it, taking into account the traditions and practices of your denomination or church grouping.

Distribute the coloured flames to the group and ask them to meditate for a few minutes on the passage they have just studied. Ask them to consider in what ways they are like Peter before the coming of the Holy Spirit, and in what ways they hope to be like the Peter of Acts 2.

Invite them to write or draw on their flames their ideas for how they would like to change under the power of the Spirit – especially in their witness to others.

As they are completed, display the flames high on the walls – symbolising the Spirit in the room. Now, together, move around the room reading each flame. At each one, stop and spend some minutes laying hands on and praying for the person who wrote that flame. As a group, offer short prayers inviting the Spirit into that person's life. Feel free to use scripture, including the text of Acts 2, to help your prayers.

OR

Pentecost painting
Spend time looking at some images of works of art that have been created by artists inspired by Pentecost. A number are available to look at on the Internet, or you could use art books from the library. If you can, look at a contemporary portrayal of the Acts 2 scene created in wonderful washes of vibrant blues and yellows by the artist Elizabeth Wang. Her *Descent of the Holy Spirit at Pentecost* can be seen at www.radiantlight.org.uk/art_gallery or bought online as a postcard. Discuss how the paintings make you feel. Have any of these images changed your mental picture

of what happened to the followers of Jesus in that house in Jerusalem? Have any of the artists conveyed a sense of the power of the Holy Spirit?

 Reaching out

Bible translation game

You will need: photocopies of page 39 giving the game, the clue sets and the key. Cut the foreign words at the top into strips and shuffle them. If you have a large group you may want to divide people into several smaller groups, in which case you will need to make extra sets of photocopies.

The aim of this activity is to establish the importance of understanding the gospel in a language you know well. It also provides an opportunity to reflect on how fortunate we are to have the Bible in our native tongue. If any of the group speak Portuguese or Spanish they may find the translation quite easy so ask them to hold back!

Before you start the activity read this to the group:

- Imagine that you only recently heard the Christian message for the first time. A foreign man visited your town and explained to you the importance of repentance and belief in Jesus quoting to you something called Acts 2:38,39 from a big book called the Bible. Here is your situation:

1   You can't remember everything he said, although you thought it was interesting at the time.

2   You decide to try and find out about this big book for yourself but the Bible is not available in your language.

3   A friend has found Acts 2:38,39 for you to read in a different language – but the words are jumbled.

Now give your group a set of game slips. Explain that their task is to try to arrange the verses into the correct order. And strictly no using English Bibles to help you!

After a few minutes the group will probably be finding it quite hard to arrange the Portuguese correctly. At this point, stop the group and say:

- An elderly Christian woman who recently came to live in your town has translated some words for you.

Give out **Clue set 1**. If the group is still struggling, give out **Clue set 2** and then **Clue set 3**. Finally, when they have their finished Bible verses, give them the **Key** to check their answer. If you have time you could discuss the following questions:

1   How did you feel when you had no clues to help you arrange the Bible verse?

2   At what point do you think you were able fully to understand the meaning of the verse?

3   What are the implications for those who can't read the Bible in their language today? How must they feel when an accurate translation is produced?

Spend some time praying for those involved in Bible translation work. Remember in your prayers those who cannot read the Bible in a language they understand well.

Note: More ideas, statistics and information are available from Wycliffe Bible Translators at www.wycliffe.org.uk

OR

Praying from the local to the global
You will need: a local street map; an atlas or a globe (all optional).

Ask a member of the group to read Acts 1:8. This verse is a succinct introduction to the rest of the book of Acts. It describes how the message of Jesus was going to move from the local (Jerusalem), to the regional (Samaria), to the national (all Judea) and to the international (the ends of the earth).

Using this progression as a model, pray together that the gospel of Jesus would go out from your town to your city or region, to your country and throughout the world. Emphasise the idea by praying over the open maps.

OR

The Spirit comes with fire
If you didn't use this activity described earlier in the **Touching God** part of the session, you could use it here.

 Digging deeper

Give each person a copy of the bookmark on page 58 to take home, with encouragement to use it during the coming week.

THE EASIEST QUIZ – Player 1

Firstly, listen as Player 2 reads you short phrases in the correct order that will complete these sentences below. Without talking or asking them any questions, listen as carefully as you can and fill in the gaps with the 'answers'.

You'll need to _____ to go surfing!

Paying _____ is quite expensive for a pub meal.

We visited the jungles of central Africa in search of _____.

Phew! _____! I've been playing football all morning.

Obviously, a bird uses _____ to fly.

The two sides agreed to a ceasefire and renewed _____.

Male players at Wimbledon need to wear a white shirt, white shorts and _____.

'The Atlantic,' said the geography teacher, 'is _____.'

I'd really fancy _____ with my mulled wine.

Dad, you're meeting my boyfriend tonight. Please _____!

Now, the tables are turned. Read this list of phrases out to Player 2. Speak clearly and naturally as you would in normal conversation. Give Player 2 time to write down their answer between each phrase.

1	may cup	6	grape written
2	plump eye	7	point of you
3	some others	8	scarf ace
4	York rhymes	9	key bout
5	field red full	10	grey day

THE EASIEST QUIZ – Player 2

Firstly, read this list of phrases for Player 1. Speak clearly and naturally as you would in normal conversation. Give Player 1 time to write down their answer between each phrase.

1	get aboard	6	pea stalks
2	sick squid	7	why choose
3	grey tapes	8	a notion
4	iced ink	9	a mint spy
5	it swings	10	bean ice

Now listen as Player 1 reads you short phrases in the correct order that will complete these sentences below. Without talking or asking them questions, listen and fill in the gaps.

I'm going out tonight. Time to do my hair and _____.

I'd fancy a piece of _____ and ice cream for dessert.

The headmaster had to deal with a complaint from _____.

'For _____,' said the judge, 'I am sending you to jail!'

Hello, Mr Smith. I can't come to work today as I've got the 'flu. I _____.

And, as usual in the Olympics, England, Scotland, Northern Ireland and Wales will be competing together as _____.

I disagree, sir. I see things from a completely different _____.

What was the name of that Al Pacino movie? Oh, I remember: _____.

We can't go in there. It says, private – _____.

I did really well in the exam! I got a _____.

Bible translation game

Pedro	Pois a promessa é
respondeu:	para vocês,
Arrependam-se,	para os seus fílhos
e cada um de vocês	e para todos
seja batizado	os que estão longe,
em nome do Jesus Cristo	para todos quantos
para perdão	o Senhor,
dos seus pecados,	o nosso
e receberão	Deus,
o dom do Espírito Santo.	chamar.

Clue set 1

Pedro = Peter
dom de Espírito Santo = the name of the Holy Spirit
Deus = God
em nome do Jesus Cristo = in the name of Jesus Christ
O Senhor = the Lord

Clue set 3

para vocês = for you
dos seus pecados = for your sins
para os seus fílhos = for your children
o nosso = our
e cada um de vocês = and each one of you
e para todos = and for all
os que estão longe = all who are far off
para todos quantos = for all whom

Clue set 2

respondeu = responded
e receberão = and receive
seja batizado = be baptised
Arrependam-se = repent
Pois a promessa é = So the promise is
chamar = will call
para perdão = for forgiveness

Key: Acts 2:38,39

How did you do?

Portuguese:

Pedro respondeu: Arrependam-se, e cada um de vocês seja batizado em nome do Jesus Cristo para perdão dos seus pecados, e receberão o dom do Espírito Santo. Pois a promessa é para vocês, para os seus fílhos e para todos os que estão longe, para todos quantos o Senhor, o nosso Deus, chamar.

English:

Peter responded: Repent, and each one of you be baptised in the name of Jesus Christ for forgiveness for your sins, and receive the gift of the Holy Spirit. So the promise is for you, for your children and for all who are far off, for all whom the Lord, our God, will call.

READY FOR MISSION!

TIME FOR PRAYER AND READING YOUR BIBLE

You suffer severe culture shock because of the different language, food, weather and customs
MOVE BACK 2

The local Panatina church holds a welcome celebration in honour of your arrival
MOVE FORWARD 2

Your bags weigh too much for the airline luggage allowance, and you realise you can't take everything you want to!
MOVE BACK 1

Your VISA and medical certificates for Panatina are not ready yet

Your ch
commissi
many pe
you of
MOVE

TIME FOR PRAYER AND READING YOUR BIBLE

Some retired mission partners lend you some useful equipment like mosquito nets and solar lights
MOVE FORWARD 1

You attend language training and orientation courses that prepare you for your trip to Panatina
MOVE FORWARD 2

You have to get immunisation injections to enter Panatina, but the jabs hurt and cost a lot of money!
MOVE BACK 1

**Stage 2
Gettin
Ready**

START

You pray with your pastor who encourages you to step into mission
MOVE FORWARD 4

**Stage 1
Raising
Support**

ᴍPOSSIBLE

TIME FOR PRAYER AND
READING YOUR BIBLE

The Panatina
officials suspect you are
trafficking drugs
so take your passport
and detain you

TIME FOR PRAYER AND
READING YOUR BIBLE

Good news: your
bags have not been
lost and nothing
seems broken or
missing
MOVE FORWARD 1

...arranges a
...g service and
...come to see
...he airport
...**RWARD 5**

Stage 3:
Arrival

Some food you eat
at the airport café
contains chilli
peppers that give
you a nasty tummy
bug
MOVE BACK 1

A kind Panatina lady
who speaks English
helps translate
some forms for you
MOVE FORWARD 2

Your mission
organisation says you
need more prayer and
financial backing

You see a TV report
about political
instability in
Panatina which
worries you!
MOVE BACK 1

TIME FOR PRAYER AND
READING YOUR BIBLE

You give a talk at
church about the
mission to Panatina
but nobody seems
to take interest
MOVE BACK 2

Your cell group
agrees to pray for
you when you go on
mission
MOVE FORWARD 2

You go on a
sponsored Sky Dive
to raise money
MOVE FORWARD 2

Some close friends
question your
decision to go to
Panatina which
discourages you!
MOVE BACK 2

TIME FOR PRAYER AND
READING YOUR BIBLE

8 The message proclaimed through community

Acts 11:19–30

The life of the early Christians in Antioch as recorded in Acts provides us with a challenging model of believers fully engaged in world concerns. It is a story of a multi-ethnic community reaching out with the gospel and offering practical help for those in need. This portion of scripture includes descriptions of remarkable people who remain nameless (verses 20,21), but the author, Luke, gives us a wonderful detail: 'The disciples were first called Christians at Antioch' (verse 26).

Most importantly, the passage teaches us about a God who is actively involved in wider global concerns as well as the detail of individual lives. The Church in Antioch is testament to the living and creative power of the Spirit working through people from a variety of backgrounds situated many miles from each other.

The activities in this session are designed to draw out two related themes: firstly, that God works through relationships between Christians across the world; secondly, that God works out of the giving of human and financial resources for those in need.

 Getting connected

String game

You will need: a large ball of string or yarn; a tray (optional).

This game is best played if your group has more than four people, all of whom know each other fairly well.

With the group standing in a circle, invite everyone to think about a time when someone else present has helped them – perhaps through a timely phone call, an encouraging word, email or letter or maybe through practical support.

To get the game going it is best if the leader starts. Holding onto the ball of string, briefly describe a time when someone has helped you. For example, 'Dan once helped me change a tyre on my car when I got a puncture and I was running late for an appointment.'

Keeping a tight hold of the end of the string, unroll the ball, giving it to whoever you noted as being helpful (in this case, Dan!).

Now it is Dan's turn to mention somebody who has been helpful. So, Dan may say, 'Wendy once called me and cheered me up after I had a really bad day at work!' Dan will pass the unravelling ball to Wendy, making sure to keep hold of the string he already has. Repeat this until everybody in the group has had several turns. You should be left with a mixed up web of crossing string, with the last person holding the depleted ball.

When you sense it is a good time to stop, ask everybody to take a small step back while holding on to his or her strings. This should make the strings tight like a net. Explain that the crossing strings represent our interconnected relationships with each other, demonstrated by providing help in simple ways. These bonds of friendship, love and trust enable us to work together for God's kingdom. Now, ask the group to imagine this web spread throughout the world between Christians. This huge net of millions of people is being used by God to further his kingdom in powerful ways through relief aid and other practical help, and spiritual support too.

If you want to illustrate the strength of the web visually, rest a flat object – such as a tray – on the tight strings.

OR

Bicycle parts

You will need: a bicycle.

Mission work across the world is a huge team effort. The Bible talks about the way different gifts are essential in the Church and in the kingdom. Some people feel that the part they play is not important. Perhaps they feel that the only 'real' mission work is done by super-spiritual people who work in the jungles of Borneo! **Bicycle parts** draws attention to the part we all play in taking the message out. It's essentially a modern-day illustration of 1 Corinthians 12:14–26. The activity can be used with children as part of a church service as well as in a small group.

Ask the group questions about each part of the bike such as:

• Could we move forward without wheels?

• What would happen if we didn't have a handlebar?

• What about the pedals? They're pretty small, so we probably don't need those – right?

If you have enough space, ask a volunteer to ride a few paces. See if they agree to doing it again – with the seat taken off and the brakes removed!

Explain that it is hard to move forward without wheels, handlebars or saddle. Even the small nuts and bolts are vital.

Mission work is made possible by people with different gifts and abilities who do different things in the kingdom. Even if you are not the one directly preaching the message, there are many essential ways to support the person who is. The first of these is prayer! Ask the group to think of different ways they can contribute their gifts to moving the kingdom forward.

OR

Source of blessing

Have you ever received help from an unexpected source? Discuss your experiences together.

 Living Scripture – Acts 11:19–30

You will need: photocopies of the map of the Eastern Mediterranean from page 45, one for each person; pens.

Hand out the pens and maps. Explain to the group that the passage describes the movements of many people involved in the early Church, particularly around Antioch. The map already shows one of Paul's key missionary trips around the region. Ask someone to read Acts 11:19–30 slowly. As a person or group of people is mentioned in the passage, have the group members draw lines from where they have come to where they are going. This should produce a map with many lines, similar to the web of strings in the game above.

1 What does your map tell you about how the church at Antioch began?

2 Luke, who wrote Acts, tells us in verse 26: 'The disciples were first called Christians at Antioch.' This term literally meant 'little Christs' and was probably derogatory in nature. From the passage, what characterised this early group of believers?

3 Up until this point, the early Church believers were witnessing only to Jews. Verse 20 explains that some believers from Cyprus and Cyrene began to spread the good news of Jesus to Greeks too. How would this have seemed to those Jewish believers? Are there groups of

people in our local communities today who we see as somehow 'outside' the good news of Jesus?

4   How did the Antioch believers react to the prophecy of Agabus? How is their response a challenge to us today?

5   Not all of us may be gifted with Agabus' prophetic insight about global events. However, we do have access to masses of information on the Internet and through various news media about famine, war and the state of the planet. How can we use this information to spur us to act positively on behalf of those in need?

 Touching God

Swapping cards

You will need: three blank postcards for each person; pens.

Ask each person to write on their cards examples of:

*   card 1: a material or practical resource they own that could be shared with others;

*   card 2: a spiritual gift they have that can be used to build up the Church;

*   card 3: a resource from the congregation that could help the wider community.

Remind your group that 'material resource' does not always mean money; it can mean, for example: time, a home, a bed, a car, clothes, a hot meal!

When the group has finished, let them swap their cards with others – symbolically demonstrating the sharing of our gifts. When everyone has three different cards from the ones they started with, draw the group together. Ask the group to use the suggestions on the cards to lead them in an open time of prayer – to include thanksgiving for the things God has given them; and for the resources and gifts listed to be shared and used powerfully in God's kingdom.

OR

Proclaiming in song

Worship God in music, singing joyfully about the proclamation of the message. Invite people in advance to bring musical instruments if they play them, distribute simple shakers (such as dried pulses inside empty bottles or cans) to everyone else and encourage them to choose songs on the theme. Suitable songs would include:

*   'For I'm building a people of power' – *The Source*, 109, *Songs of Fellowship*, 111, *Mission Praise*, 151.

*   'Filled with compassion' – *The Source*, 105, *Songs of Fellowship*, 716.

*   'From the sun's rising' – *The Source*, 116, *Songs of Fellowship*, 122, *Mission Praise*, 164.

 Reaching out

External input

In the Acts 11 passage, Barnabas went to another city to get Paul and brought him back to Antioch to teach the church (verses 25,26). Sometimes, the input of outsiders is useful in broadening our own vision too.

Is there someone from outside you could invite to broaden the vision of your church or home group? Perhaps you could invite a Christian from another country (maybe an international student or refugee), or a missionary with experience of another part of the world, or somebody who has worked in another culture. You could set up an event with food and information about the place they will talk about, with the aim of challenging those who attend to think about the world in new ways and to gain an understanding of the realities of church life in another place.

OR

Case study 5: Water of life

You will need: photocopies of the Interserve case study on page 55; a flipchart.

Before distributing the photocopies, give the group these three verbal clues as to what this story is about and see how quickly they can guess the topic: 'thermal movement', 'spectacular fountain', and 'irrigation pipe'.

After reading the case study, brainstorm the skills, resources or areas of expertise in the group that could be used to help others in practical ways.

 Digging deeper

Give each person a copy of the bookmark on page 58 to take home, with encouragement to use it during the coming week.

Living Scripture – Acts 11:19–30

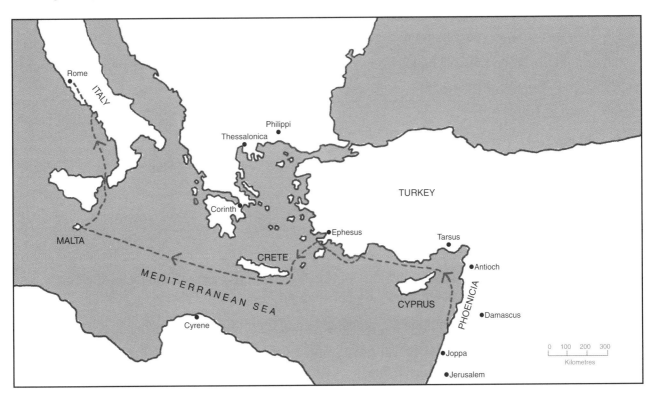

9 The glorious end of the message

Revelation 21:1–8,22; 21:22 – 22:5

These amazing verses towards the very end of the Bible give us a thrilling glimpse of the restored community of God's people living in total communion with him. The imagery is of a beautiful wedding; of a city with no darkness; of an abundant tree; of freedom from sin, pain and tears. Mission work is finished – God's people are now congregated for worship! These pictures span the message of the whole Bible by showing us a return to Eden, where all God's renewed creation live together in the New Jerusalem. The possibility of this union revolves around the work of Jesus – the bridegroom who bought the nations to be his bride.

Sometimes it is difficult to comprehend the scope of these verses. Indeed, Revelation is a mysterious book that has befuddled many a theologian through the centuries! The purpose of this study is not to miss the wood for the trees by getting bogged down in minute discussions of interpretation. Rather, hopefully, those looking at these verses will gain an understanding of:

- worship as the goal of mission;
- the prospect of eternal intimacy with God and his people from all nations;
- the Church's motivation to work at mission today.

 Getting connected

Welcome!
You will need: photocopies of page 49, cut into horizontal strips.

Give one strip to each person in the group – or two each if it's a small group.

Go around the group and ask people to say their welcome word. Everyone else must try to guess which language has been spoken.

OR

Crowd control
What is the largest crowd you have ever been in? Why were you there? How did you feel?

 Touching God

Picture the scene
Invite people to become quiet in an attitude of worship, with eyes closed. You may want to dim the lights and perhaps play gentle music in the background.

Slowly read the meditation on page 50, pausing where appropriate.

Afterwards, spend some time in prayer as a group – worshipping God and thanking him for the future vision of an eternity spent with him.

OR

Reading Revelation
Stand and read Revelation 7:9–17 together as a group, as dramatically as you can. Use the words as a launch pad for prayer, thanking and worshipping God.

Living Scripture – Revelation 21:1–8; 21:21 – 22:5.

Invite a good reader to read out the verses before tackling the questions together.

1 Many of these verses describe the intimacy of God with his people. What images from the verses do you find especially exciting? How has this intimacy of God with his people been made possible?

2 Verse 8 seems abruptly out of place. It describes the destiny of those whose lives demonstrate that they have not followed God. This raises the question of the nature of hell, a topic with which many people today are uncomfortable. And yet, from Jesus' teaching and right through the New Testament to Revelation there is a clear divide between those who – because of a belief in the saving power of Jesus' death and resurrection – have been bought into the family of God, and those who have not. What do you think of verse 8? How does its message motivate us in our witness to those who do not know Christ?

3 Look again at the verses that talk about 'the nations': specifically 21:24,26; 22:2. How is the goal and destiny of God's people described in these verses?

4 Popular notions of heaven often include bearded men with halos sitting on clouds strumming harps. How do verses 22:2,3 contradict the stereotypical picture of what life will be like there?

5 It has been said that worship is the goal of mission. In what ways do these verses spur us on in a) our own worship life? b) our desire to see others from all nations worshipping Jesus?

 ## Reaching out

Unreached people group

In the 1970s, missiologists (those who study mission) believed that there was at least one Christian from every nation in the world. Although the gospel has made great progress, today we know there are still millions who do not have the opportunity to hear about Jesus.

Find out about Unreached People Groups (UPGs) – people with no viable Christian witness. A number of websites give useful information. You could start with www.joshuaproject.net or www.missionresources.com. Select one UPG to pray for. Commit to praying for your UPG over the coming weeks, asking God to draw many from that people to the celebration of the nations.

OR

Leaves of the tree medicine

You will need: a small bottle of methylated spirit; an adhesive address label; a pen; an old handkerchief or piece of lightweight cloth such as muslin; water colour paints, or non-permanent markers.

Note: it's a good idea to practise this in advance; and be aware of safety considerations about using methylated spirit in an enclosed space.

Write on the sticky label 'Leaves of the tree medicine' and stick it to the bottle of methylated spirit.

Ask the group to think of situations in our world where there is pain: conflicts between nations, famine, disease or natural disasters. Invite them to use the paints or pens to write their thoughts onto the handkerchief or other cloth. Spend some time praying over the things that are written, asking God to bring healing.

After the prayers, read aloud Revelation 22:1,2. Remind everyone of the special powers of the tree – sourced by the water from the throne of God, yielding a crop of fruit each month of the year!

Produce your 'Leaves of the tree medicine'. Pour a small amount onto each of the areas with writing and rub the cloth until the paint or ink disappears.

Close in prayer, thanking God that he promises one day to heal the hurt of the nations and provide a final solution to the pain and evil in the world.

Digging deeper

Give each person a copy of the bookmark on page 58 to take home, with encouragement to use it during the coming week.

Welcome!

Witaj	Polish
Karibu	Kiswahili [South East Africa]
Hwangyong-hamnida	Korean
Tavtai moril	Mongolian
Qaimarutin	Inuktitut [Alaskan Eskimo]
Merhaba	Arabic
Bem-vindo	Portuguese
Kia orana	Maori [Cook Islands]
Aloha mai	Hawaiian
Bienvenue	French
Swaagatam	Hindi [India]
Baruch haba	Hebrew

Picture the scene

Picture the scene. The finest athletes of the world are assembled for the world's most prestigious sporting event – the Olympic Games, the pinnacle of sporting glory. Thousands of people are sitting in a huge stadium waiting for the opening ceremony to begin. Millions, maybe billions, are watching on glowing TV screens around the world. Everyone is poised in expectation. The floodlights beam down onto the empty track. And then – it starts!

Theatrical dancers create spectacular formations… dramatic music booms to a crescendo… screens blaze with colour… hundreds of costumed children sing… important dignitaries deliver speeches… cameras flash across the assembled masses.

Then… what everyone has been waiting for! The competing nations march in… dressed in national costumes, smiling, waving… the proudest moment of their lives. And, at the front of each group, a chosen athlete waves their national flag.

You know those who have made it here will never forget this day. At the finale a lone runner comes in, jogs up the steps and lights the Olympic torch. Fireworks cascade into the night sky… the noise is deafening as the crowd goes wild… Let the games begin!

Now… picture another scene. Thousands… certainly millions… perhaps even billions of people… assembled for a magnificent ceremony. And you are there!

There is music… beautiful symphonies of exquisite music and incredible choruses of voices… unlike anything you or anyone else has heard before. This is certainly not the Olympic Games. This is much bigger. What is the purpose of this gathering, you wonder? Is it some kind of wedding feast?

There are people from many different backgrounds and every corner of the world here… from every tribe, nation and language, all dressed in white… all shouting and singing and dancing and laughing. Their faces display a pure radiance. You can see that their entire lives have been leading up to this very moment. Nobody here will ever forget this.

And then – it starts! A dazzling light! So overwhelmingly bright! A mighty roar like the sound of crashing waves… And the bridegroom appears – shining – and everywhere is light. No need for fireworks or floodlights or cameras or special effects. There is no more night. Darkness no longer exists. And the bride is the assembled nations – resplendent, honoured and glorified. Time does not matter anymore. You know this will never end.

This is a celebration to which everyone is invited. The party lasts for ever… and you are there… in the holy city, the New Jerusalem! You cannot contain your excitement! And you and everyone else cries in a loud voice: 'Salvation belongs to our God who sits on the throne and to the Lamb! Amen! Praise and glory and wisdom and thanks and honour and power and strength be to our God for ever and ever! Amen!'

Case Studies

1

A better understanding

One morning I came across a man who had spent the early part of the day hunting on the Aammiq wetland, which A Rocha is working to protect. On his belt were hanging eight different species of bird, including black-headed bunting, little egret, red-backed shrike, little crake, and great snipe (a globally threatened species and a large reason for the Aammiq Marsh's importance). He saw me, and I approached him.

Pause for discussion.

With my limited Arabic, I tried to explain that he shouldn't be hunting in this area. Unfortunately, I was mostly ignored and he happily continued hunting just outside the protected area. This situation caused me to think about how we can make a difference to people's views and their treatment of God's creation. It is certainly not our policy to run after every hunter and try to convince them that what they're doing is wrong. Rather, we feel we can make a greater difference through our environmental education programme – by giving children the opportunity to change their attitudes towards what God has made.

During a typical field trip, children have the opportunity to explore God's world through a pair of binoculars, a magnifying glass, or by catching small animals and insects on the land and in the water. Our desire is that each child will go away with a better understanding of creation, and why it is important to protect and care for it. We hope they will see that the different birds, animals and insects are not merely objects to be destroyed, but rather part of God's wonderful and diverse creation, which he loves and wants to see thrive.

Above everything else we hope that these children will gain a greater understanding of God as Creator, and – because of this – draw nearer to him.

2

Woman to woman

Fatma was born into a rural community in the Middle East. At the age of 21, as I pursued my cherished career, Fatma travelled halfway around the world to join the household of her little-known husband, a British-born cousin from her country.

Fatma is to me 'the lady who always smiles.' Her smile flickered briefly even that day we became friends. She came to English class, her face black with bruising. Her nose had been bleeding and she had been crying. Her smallest daughter clung to her.

Slowly a life story unfolded... of her mother-in-law's hatred... her husband's slide into drug abuse... her rough treatment by her sisters-in-law... the rising cost of marital violence. Heavily pregnant with another child, she was fearful, yet could not face the shame of leaving her husband.

What could I – a single, childless woman from a secure family and a different culture – do or say? Prayer, hugs and tears seemed the best language. The words, 'I have called you to be there' echoed in my mind and they have never left me.

Fatma disappeared for a while, staying with a brother until her husband's anger subsided. Then pressure from the community drew her back. She no longer lives with his family, but things have got no better. Some of her family say, 'Leave him'. Others say, 'Think of the shame and keep quiet.' I am asked what I think. What should I say?

Fatma is pale when next I arrive at her house. Mysterious things have been happening. The air seems thick with an evil presence. 'Something' has tried to attack Fatma's son.

Gently, but with increasing urgency, I begin to speak of the power of Jesus; how Jesus told demons to run and they ran; how Jesus cared for people whose lives were torn apart by Satan.

Fatma's response to the name of Jesus is abrupt and decisive. 'No thank you! The wise man at the end of the street will know what to do. He has charms that can help us. He can give us water we can drink, mixed with words from a book that protects us.'

A picture comes to my mind. Fatma is frantically digging in muddy puddles, searching for water, while the clear, pure river of life flows beside her.

My friendship with Fatma continues to develop through pain and laughter. We are learning that we are not so different. Really, only one thing divides us: though I am no better than she, and am often challenged by her religious zeal, I know for sure that I am going to heaven. I want her to be there too, to know Jesus' healing, to find living water. After all, she's my sister!

3

The human face of HIV

Kavita is 30, married, with three children under the age of six. Having gone against family norms, she married the man of her choice and was ostracised by her family. Soon after her marriage, it became clear that the man she had given up so much for was HIV positive and consequently she found herself ostracised for a second time.

Her husband had been a rickshaw driver until his health started to fail and, once the full implications of his situation dawned on him, he turned to alcohol. This in turn led to abuse.

As if that wasn't enough, Kavita lives with the knowledge that at least one of her children is also HIV positive, and the whole burden of supporting the family financially falls on her shoulders. She sells flower garlands just outside her slum community, earning a very meagre income. Because of her family's ill health and the abuse in her home, Kavita is a desperate person looking for a way out.

Purnata Bhavan (The House of Wholeness) is a care community for women and children infected and affected by HIV. It gives people like Kavita a place to live and a variety of educational and training opportunities in a caring environment, providing hope for the future.

Purnata Bhavan was established by Oasis India, to whom several Interserve Partners are seconded.

4

Should I stay or should I go?

Mark and Teresa Pietroni are both medical doctors and Interserve Partners who have been living and working in Bangladesh for ten years. Here, Mark shares some thoughts about the question of calling. How do you know when you are called to leave everything that is secure and stable to live and work in a different culture?

Interviewer How can someone know whether to go or whether to stay?

Mark I would say that unless you actively consider working overseas, the chances are you will never end up overseas! Our experience was that we had been working for five years in the UK, earning good salaries as doctors, and we started to think about having children. We realised that if we had delayed considering working overseas much longer then it would have been too difficult to leave. We would have moved into a nice house and been more settled and so on. But because we were actively considering mission, we left ourselves open to hearing God's call.

So, I encourage everybody, whatever your profession, to really ask the question, 'What is it that God wants me to do with my life at this moment?'

Interviewer Another area of concern for missionaries appears to be, 'What possible use can I be with so much need around?' Did you address that question?

Mark If you are wondering whether you may be of any use or make a difference overseas, I would encourage you in two ways. First of all, I would say that if God calls you to work overseas, then he has work for you to do, and that work is important to him. And if that work is important to him, then it's important that you do it. Whether or not you see the results in front of your eyes either in physical terms or even in spiritual terms, if it's the work God has called you to, then it's the work you should do. And I think that's the bottom line. Secondly, I would say that anybody who has had a western education, who has been taught 'problem solving', who's been taught to analyse, who's been taught to apply the knowledge they have to a difficult situation, is of tremendous value in many overseas contexts.

Interviewer How about the question, 'Are my skills sufficient for the work I might be doing?'

Mark It doesn't really matter what your professional skills and qualifications are, or even if you feel you have none, in the environment of the under-developed world; just what you bring with you as educational background is effective and powerful. Whatever work you do, you will always end up in teaching and training people just to think. Often people overseas with an educational background in which they have not been encouraged to ask questions or take initiative or 'problem solve', find it very difficult to apply their knowledge to new situations. So, anybody who has been through a western education can be effective, particularly in south Asia, whatever their professional or educational background.

5

Water of life

There is a lot of water in Nepal but, as most of it falls in the monsoon season, it isn't always in the right place at the right time! That's why, between two hills, a long irrigation pipe has been built – a real feat of engineering. And the man behind it is Interserve Partner Peter Millais. He says, 'When the wind blows, the pipe moves slightly. When you fill it with water, it sags. When it's empty, it expands with the temperature. When you fill it with water, it cools again. That's thermal movement – so designing the joints was a major challenge.'

Was there ever a point at which he thought it might not work?

'I did have visions of a spectacular fountain if a joint failed and water under pressure was spurting out. I took the project on from somebody else and if I'd been asked to do it from scratch I'd probably have said, "No, you shouldn't attempt it." But we were committed, and I began to see that prayer is vital to my work as well as in the rest of my life. Certainly a lot of prayer went into that project, and it's good to see that God gave me the wisdom to produce a workable design.'

The pipe really has changed things for the farmers. Before irrigation, they could only plant maize and millet. Now they can make paddy fields and grow their own rice and vegetables too.

Bookmarks

3
The message for the least deserving

What more can you find out about Jonah and his book?

See if you can get hold of some commentaries and try to answer these questions:

When was the book of Jonah written, and who wrote it?

Who were the Ninevites? What were they like?

In terms of biblical characters, who were Jonah's contemporaries?

Is it possible Jonah was really swallowed by a fish?

In what context is Jonah mentioned in the New Testament?

2
The message of blessing

Read both Psalm 104 and 105 and reflect on the majesty of God's involvement in our world. And then pray for the world:

Thank you, Father,
that you set the earth
on its foundations
so that it can never be moved…

We ask you to
bring forth food from the earth:
wine that gladdens the heart of man,
oil to make his face shine,
and bread to sustain his heart…

1
Creation
– the message of hope

The writers of Proverbs often draw on the natural world for the lessons they pass on. Meditate on the lessons we can learn from God's creation in these verses.

Proverbs 6:6–8

Proverbs 26:1–3,17

Proverbs 28:1,15

Proverbs 30:24–28

Proverbs 30:29–31

• Can you think of any of proverbs in current use that are drawn from nature?

Bookmarks

6
The Great Commission – getting the message out!

The Great Commission is often read or quoted in isolation and much is made of it being Jesus' last recorded words in Matthew's Gospel. However, the message of the Great Commission – the authority of Jesus, the promise of his presence and the task set before his followers to make disciples of all nations – are recurring themes throughout Matthew. Some theologians see the Great Commission as key to understanding the whole of that Gospel. Take time to read these passages in Matthew in the light of the Great Commission:

1:22,23

8:5–13

9:1–8

11:27–30

21:23–27

5
Training manual for messengers

Matthew 10 was not just a blueprint for the disciples of Jesus' day but a model of discipleship for subsequent generations. Look in the Acts chapters listed below and ask yourself:

- How did Jesus' words as recorded in Matthew 10 prove to be a good indication of things to come?

- How would Jesus' words have been an encouragement to the early Christians in the situations they faced?

- What lessons do we learn for ourselves?

  Acts 3
  Acts 16
  Acts 19
  Acts 21
  Acts 25 and 26

4
The message in person – Jesus!

Simeon's prophecy talks about how Jesus will be a 'light for revelation to the Gentiles' (Luke 2:32). Take time to look at the ways Jesus interacted with and spoke about those who were not Israelites.

The Samaritan woman (John 4:1–42)

- Does Jesus answer her questions directly? What was the result of the encounter?

The centurion (Matthew 8:5–13)

- Are there any lessons about our own faith we can learn from the centurion?

The parable of the good Samaritan (Luke 10:25–37)

- How do you think this story would have sounded to the Jews of Jesus' day?

The Canaanite woman (Matthew 15:21–28)

- Why was Jesus' initial response to the Canaanite woman seemingly negative?

Bookmarks

9

The glorious end of the message

The book of Revelation contains echoes of many things written about earlier in the Bible. The verses we have been looking at in chapters 21 and 22 both elaborate and intensify earlier Old Testament Scriptures. Spend time looking at the way John's visions in Revelation complement these prophecies:

Isaiah 56:1–8
Isaiah 65:17–25
Jeremiah 7:5–7
Daniel 7:13,14

• Can you think of any other passages?

Thank God for his marvellous Word. Meditate on God's great promises of restoration and renewal.

8

The message proclaimed through community

Think about the four G's of engaging with our world as you investigate these Bible verses and pray about whether God is speaking to you about any of them.

Get on our knees and pray –
1 Timothy 2:1–8

Gather information for action –
Nehemiah 2

Give out of our own resources –
Luke 21:1–4

Go when we are called –
Matthew 9:35–38

7

Power to communicate the message

The story of languages through the Bible makes a fascinating study. From Genesis to Revelation,

the variety of languages people speak has been used by God to humble humanity as well as empower them. Spend some time this week looking at these key passages. As you do, ask yourself:

• Why has God given us different languages?

• What do we learn about God's heart for all peoples?

• Do we learn anything about how God communicates his character to us?

Genesis 11:1–9
Psalm 19
Mark 16:15–20
Acts 2:1–11
Revelation 7:9–17

Games

Game 1

Secret mission

You will need: a world map or atlas; photocopies of the kit list on page 62.

This short activity would be a great icebreaker for an evening or event centred on world mission.

Inform the group that they are about to embark on a secret mission. They could be sent to any part of the world as messengers of the good news of Jesus.

Take it in turns to go around the group. Each contestant must first choose the destination for their outreach. They do this by opening the atlas randomly and pointing to the page (without looking). If the page does not have a map on or they have chosen the middle of the ocean, repeat until they point to land somewhere in the world.

Based on their destination, candidates now have to choose three essential items from the kit list, explaining why they see them as essential. Invite group participation in the discussion over whether the items are really suitable. For example, could you really take a Bible into a Communist country? Would you need sunglasses in Scotland?

Finally, ask the group for one person they could call for advice about this trip. Who would it be and why?

Game 2

History comes to life!

You will need: a variety of props and costumes for people to try – such as hats, cloaks, walking sticks, scarves.

The history of mission is the story of God working in extraordinary ways in the lives of ordinary people. These lives can be a challenge and inspiration to us today. This drama activity draws on this rich heritage of mission and is suitable for small or large groups of people of all ages. As well as being a lot of fun – especially if you use props and costumes – it teaches some memorable and true stories of how God used people from the past to further his kingdom.

The aim of this activity is for your group to organise and perform a short play on the life of a Christian from the past used by God in communicating the good news. Split your group up into five smaller groups or pairs. If your group meets regularly and are fairly independently motivated, ask them to research this themselves (of course, giving them some advance warning). Otherwise you may have to be responsible for research, bringing to the meeting ideas and information about five godly men or women of the past.

Ask the groups to organise a five-minute sketch based on the historical figure they have chosen or been assigned. They can use props or costumes to add to their sketch. The completed sketch could be a speedy overview of their character's entire life or just an account of one or two key incidents.

Missionaries often have the most riveting life stories, but don't feel you should be limited to traditional Christian heroes such as John Wesley or William Carey. Many great heroes of mission have been very normal people doing very normal jobs. The American pastor John Piper has a collection of excellent biographical talks about great Christian men from the past. They are free to download and listen to at www.desiringgod.org/ResourceLibrary/Biographies/

Don't make the mistake of overlooking women – often the unsung heroes of mission – or less well known people from other countries. A good book to get you started is *People my Teachers* by John Stott (Candle Books, 2002).

Game 3

Mission Impossible

You will need: an A3 photocopy of the Mission Impossible board game from pages 40 and 41, if possible pasted onto a piece of thick card; counters; dice.

Mission Impossible is a board game that simulates the process of getting ready to embark on mission to the fictional country of Panatina in South America. The game could be used as an icebreaker in a small group setting, as an activity with young people or even as pre-training for those finding out about being involved in mission, either as supporters of others or as short-term or long-term field workers themselves. The game raises some interesting issues about the process of going on mission.

All players begin at the Start square and take turns to roll the dice and move round the board. The first player to the Ready for Mission square is the winner.

Discussion questions at the completion of the game:

1   What problems did you encounter trying to get ready for mission?

2   Did you ever feel as if you were going around in circles?

3   Was the experience of preparing for mission the same for everyone in the game?

4   How important was the involvement and interest of close Christian friends? And the local church?

5   Think about any mission partners you know. Does the game simulate the kinds of struggles they may have gone through, or are still going through?

6   Think about the fictional country of Panatina in South America. What are the pros and cons of going into another country to engage in mission work?

7   'What a nightmare – I'm never going on mission!' or 'What an adventure – when can I go on mission?' Which reaction quote sums up how you feel after playing Mission Impossible?

Game 4

Mission simulator

You will need: photocopies of pages 63 and 64, cut into three, as indicated; a pack of playing cards; assorted hats, ties and woolly coats to distinguish people groups from one another (optional). If you are feeling really adventurous you could use face paints, masks or more elaborate costumes.

The good news of Jesus has been travelling the world since the resurrection. This game simulates the way mission work often starts in small ways but can lead to big results. It also shows the kinds of obstacles that may be faced when approaching a new people group with the gospel. It highlights the sorts of solutions that can occur when more and more of God's people are engaged in taking the good news into the world.

This game is best played with a larger mixed-sex group. The game will probably not last more than 10 minutes but it can lead to fruitful discussion that can go on much longer.

One person needs to be selected before the game begins to take the part of 'Christian', eager to tell the good news of Jesus to more and more people, persistent even if not always meeting with success!

The rest of the group should be divided into three equal groups and given the photocopied description of the people group they represent. Ask one person from each group to read the instructions to the rest, making sure they do not reveal the information to anybody else or 'Christian'. Remind them that they are to obey the cultural rules of their people group diligently!

Place the pack of cards on a table. Explain to everyone that the cards represent the message of the good news of Jesus Christ. 'Christian' should pick up one card for himself, since he already knows the gospel. Tell 'Christian' that his or her goal is for everyone in the room to have their own card – that is, for everyone to have accepted the good news of Jesus. Once a person has accepted a card they become a new Christian convert and can be enlisted to help in distributing other cards. If a card is rejected, 'Christian' or one of the recent converts must go back to the table and pick up a new card to give to somebody else each time. Let the game begin!

Discussion

After the game, you may wish to have a discussion about some of the dynamics of mission that the simulator highlights. Start with a question for 'Christian': was it easy giving out cards at the beginning, on your own? Then go on to discuss: What, if anything, do we learn from this simulation about how the good news of Jesus goes forward into the world?

'Christian' should not to be thought of as the stereotypical hard-hat-wearing, nineteenth-century missionary to Africa! Telling the good news of Jesus is something we are all encouraged to do today in our neighbourhoods, workplaces, schools, and with friends and family – even if we don't think of ourselves as missionaries. Did anything in the game encourage you (or discourage you!) in this task of taking the good news of Jesus out to the people you know?

Secret mission – kit list

1 Strong shoes

2 Flashlight

3 Heavy-duty sleeping bag

4 Tent

5 Solar panel

6 Land Rover

7 Swiss army knife

8 Bottle of fresh water

9 Mosquito repellent

10 Bible

11 Mobile phone

12 Portable rubber boat

13 French dictionary

14 Wardrobe of smart clothes

15 Sunglasses

The Zakminski

Costume: large winter coats.

The Zakminski people of the People's Republic of Zakministan live in a cold, harsh climate in some place not unlike Siberia. Often starved for attention, the Zakminski people are very happy to accept gifts from any strangers. In fact, if somebody were to give them a card they might give them a huge bear hug to say 'thank you'.

It is important to remember, however, that Zakminski men work 16 hours a day in underground mines to get coal to keep the cities of Zakministan warm at night. Women do most other jobs including rearing children, cleaning and cooking. Because of these work patterns, the Zakminski have a very pronounced gender divide. A spirit of distrust honed over many decades exists between the sexes. Men claim women do not understand how hard it is for them to work in the coal mines. Women accuse men of being lazy, not helping with household chores or child rearing.

Things in Zakministan have got so bad that no man will ever accept a gift from a woman, and no woman will ever accept a gift from a man. This rule also applies to any stranger bearing gifts!

The QWeRtYUiOP tRibe Of nORth afRiCa

Costume: crazy hats or masks or face paint. Choose one member of the group to be the chief.

The Qwertyuiop tribe of North Africa are a very proud people with a rich cultural history. Everyone in the tribe will refuse any gift given by anyone outside the tribe on the basis that they are perfectly able to provide for their own needs as they have deep wells, good crops and lots of cattle. For example, if somebody were to offer them a card, they would shout, 'Hokuwanga!' They might even throw it to the ground, stamping on it several times.

But the tribe hold their chief in high esteem for his wisdom and benevolent ways. And if they saw their chief accept a gift from a stranger they would happily copy him too, accepting any similar gifts that might come their way.

Surprisingly for an African tribe, the chief can be either male or female and he/she does not wear any outstanding costume, preferring to look just the same as all of his/her people. The chief of the Qwertyuiop is very intrigued by new ideas and is prepared to accept straightaway any gift a stranger may bring.

The Street Rebels

Costume: necktie or cord tied around the forehead like a bandana.

The Street Rebels are an inner city group of young people. They are not a bad lot really, though they feel they are often misunderstood. They are suspicious of outsiders because other people always seem to have it in for them. In fact, every time anyone has offered anything to a Street Rebel they feel it usually comes with strings attached. Street Rebels respect other Street Rebels though, because they are all mates and have had the same tough upbringing.

When strangers bring gifts to a Street Rebel, the gift would be refused for the first three times it was offered. For example, if an outsider were to bring a card, a Street Rebel would throw the card straight in the air shouting, 'No way, man!'

But if a stranger came a fourth time with a card, a Street Rebel would respect this persistence and accept it. And if another member of the Street Rebels came offering cards they would accept it straight away without hesitation. If a Street Rebel did accept a card from someone, their way of saying thanks would be to give the card-giver a hearty handshake while saying, 'Sweet!'

Events

Event 1

WORLD CINEMA

You will need: a DVD of an international film (see suggestions below); popcorn and other nibbles; drinks.

Movies are perhaps the primary medium for, and source of, twenty-first century stories. If you don't like films, then somebody close to you is bound to, and they will probably enjoy talking about the plots and characters of films at some length. In recent years some very good films have been made from, or about, other parts of the world. The aim of this activity is to help people discover the realities of other parts of the world, and call people to pray.

A note of caution: Be aware! Some of these films are graphic and contain difficult and challenging material. Always watch a film before you show it to a group to gauge its content and suitability.

For each film you watch ask some basic questions:

1   Which characters did you relate to? Why?

2   What themes – perhaps of love, hope, sacrifice – came out in the story?

3   Were there any Christians in the films? What were they doing and what were they like?

4   Did you learn anything about another part of the world?

5   As a Christian, what is your response to the movie? What would you have done if you were the lead character(s)? Does it challenge you to pray – if so, what about?

Here are some films that could be used and some of the issues they touch on:

> *In This World* – refugees/poverty/the Middle East
>
> *Central Station* – Brazil/South America/orphans
>
> *Abouna* – North Africa/Islam
>
> *Goodbye Lenin* – Germany/politics/family
>
> *Secrets and Lies* – London/race/class/forgiveness
>
> *Lost in Translation* – Japan/isolation/love
>
> *Hotel Rwanda* – war/genocide/Africa
>
> *Spirited Away* – Asia/Eastern philosophy
>
> *Crash* – Los Angeles, USA/race/class
>
> *Rabbit Proof Fence* – Australia/race/family/politics

Pointers for success:

• Pray for the evening before you start – that God will use the film as a means to give us a concerned heart for his world.

• Be sure to provide popcorn!

• Leave time for a discussion.

Film nights can be adapted to your group's interests and style. For example, you could watch the latest DVD blockbuster, followed by discussion, as a social event, inviting friends who don't usually attend home group.

Event 2

THE MESSAGE IN THE WORLD FAIR

This is a way of involving people in finding out more about what God is doing across the globe. Because this involves everyone in the group, it means less work for leaders and others get to learn initiative! You could set aside a whole evening for the fair, with all the presentations happening on the same night. Or, you could make this a 10–15 minute slot in your group time over a period, as people take turns to present. Of course, the idea can also be adapted to be a part of a church service for the whole congregation.

The task for each person is to research a project, a mission partner, a country or a political situation under the title, 'The message in the world'. They need to include:

- background information;

- at least one story of how the message of Christ has gone out in that part of the world;

- prayer requests.

Encourage everyone to use their imagination to prepare their presentation – through craft, video, song, costume, ethnic foods and so on. You could also consider inviting a speaker to talk about how things really are 'on the ground'. Most mission agencies have regional representatives who are usually more than happy to come to give a presentation.

Event 3

Giving something back to the takeaway

You don't have to travel the world to meet people from other cultures! Students, migrants, refugees and business people from scores of different countries are present in all our major towns and cities. One group of people who provide a valuable service, but are often taken for granted, are restaurant and takeaway staff.

Almost every town centre has a curry house, a Chinese restaurant, Italian eatery or kebab shop. But have you ever made a point of finding out a bit about who makes your food? You may not know, for example, that in the UK almost all so-called 'Indian' food is actually made by Bangladeshis. And you may not realise that a lot of takeaway staff live on the same premises as their restaurants, in one or two rooms above the outlet. Many of them rarely form relationships with those in the society they serve. What's more, many of these people come from countries with little Christian witness. They are examples of a mission field on your doorstep.

Buy a takeaway to enjoy together as a social evening for your group. Using the Internet or an atlas, find out a bit about the country the food comes from. Pray before eating your food, thanking God for those who made it. Discuss together ways you can reach out to them and take an interest in them. Here are some ideas to get you started:

- Keep buying from the same takeaway so you build rapport with the staff.

- Send them a Christmas card to say thank you for their work.

- Find out about their national and cultural holidays – for example, send the Chinese takeaway a card at Chinese New Year.

- Arrive early to pick up your food and chat to the staff while you wait. Ask them about themselves, where they are from, their families, their food, their country, their religion, their sports teams etc.

- Ask them to teach you a few greetings in their language.

- Importantly, look at the example of how Jesus treated people who were outsiders in his society (see John 4).

Pointers for success:

- Within your group, appoint one person to take particular responsibility for maintaining the link.

- Stay accountable as to how you are doing.

- Be prepared to put in considerable effort over a long time. It may seem daunting!

- Be prepared for disappointments. Your new friends may be shy or suspicious at first. Barriers, especially of language, may be very high.

- Remember that small things – such as calling them by their name next time you visit, or speaking intelligently about their hometown or country – will probably pleasantly surprise them. It's unlikely other customers will ever have made the effort! These little touches go a long way.

- Keep praying for those you meet in your local takeaway, asking God to give you an attitude of love and humility towards them, and his Spirit of wisdom as you attempt conversations. Pray that God will ultimately give you opportunities to explain more about his Son Jesus.

Event 4

Football fun

Do you know that thousands of people today love to go to big communal meeting places on Sundays to worship and sing songs? Some go to church – and others go to football matches!

Football is avidly followed by billions of people across the world. It is a truly universal language, especially for men. Below are two ideas about how you can incorporate aspects of this universal language into your services and outreach.

A note of caution: Incorporating football into church activities can be difficult as those who are fans may talk only about football for hours – and never about God! Meanwhile, those who are not fans may become bored very quickly. Also, some Christians have strong views about the place of football in church. You should consult with your church leaders or your group if you have any doubts.

1. Football-themed service
During the World Cup or another major football tournament, why not have a football-themed church service? We did this at my church. All those at the front wore football shirts from different countries of the world. You could sing football chants for Jesus! In our service, the main aim was to show that, although football can be fun, it does not provide lasting joy or real solutions. We compared the spectacular fanfare of a World Cup final to the far greater meeting of the nations in heaven.

2. Football outreach
Organise a social evening for your small group when an important football match is being broadcast

on TV. Invite friends who are fans of the teams involved. Prepare suitable snacks and drinks.

Informally or formally, use the half-time break to begin a discussion about the place of football in our lives. Perhaps explain how you view football from the perspective of your faith. Or, you could speak the 'language' of football by mentioning the testimonies of famous Christian footballers. Ask your friends about their interest in football. Don't pressure them with too many questions – after all, you did invite them to watch football, not have a huge academic debate! Maintain the relationships after the evening and continue your discussions if you get the opportunity. Perhaps follow up by going to watch a live football match with your friends.

Event 5

Multi-Sensory pub quiz

Why not organise a pub quiz about the world? But rather than just have a list of questions on a sheet about capital cities, try creating a Multi-Sensory pub quiz! Ask the group to invite friends who don't usually come to church, especially if they are interested in travel and finding out about the world.

This activity takes a lot of preparation, depending on which rounds you want to include in your quiz. Divide your group into pairs or small teams. The teams confer to choose an answer they all agree on. Some ideas you could use or adapt would be:

1   **Tasting and smelling round** Blindfold contestants and let them sniff and sample simple dishes, ingredients or fruit from different parts of the world. Their task is to guess correctly the country the food comes from.

2   **Touching and seeing round** Let contestants examine some fabrics from different parts of the world. Their task is to guess correctly the country the cloth came from.

3   **Postcard round** Using postcards that have been sent to you from different parts of the world, let the group see the pictures on the front, but blank out the destination. They could get one point for guessing the correct country, and two points for choosing the right city or town.

4   **Listening round** Play short clips of music from different parts of the world. Contestants have to guess where the music is from.

At the end of the evening provide a prize for the winning team.

Prayer Activities

Prayer activity 1

A house of prayer for all nations

You will need: lots of sofa cushions; photocopies of the top part of page 73.

The closing chapters of Isaiah contain some glorious passages that describe the suffering servant and the promises of God for the future of the nations. Isaiah 56 contains beautiful verses about the ultimate international festival – a continuous worshipful, prayerful party at the throne of God. This activity is more of an illustration or icebreaker. It would work well in a youth group or an all-age church service. The aim is to draw attention, in a fun way, to the 'house of prayer for all nations'.

Ask the group to try and build a 'cushion fort' into which one person can fit, lying down. When they have finished, ask them to build a fort inside which the whole group can fit. For this one you could use some chairs or the wall to help make it possible.

When they have successfully completed the task, ask if they would like to build another 'cushion fort'. Explain that this is a house talked about in the Bible. Give out the photocopies and ask somebody to read the verses. Have an informal discussion about the kind of house being talked about:

- How big would this house need to be?
- How many nations are there in the world?
- How many cushions would we need?

Spend some time meditating on the verses. Thank God that his blessings and promise extend to us today and that we are invited to the house of prayer for all nations.

Prayer activity 2

Three-stage prayer

This simple prayer activity is appropriate for the beginning or end of a group meeting. You could precede this with a suitable Scripture reading, such as a psalm, that will help focus minds on God.

Ask the group to stand in a circle facing each other. Everyone is to lift their hands up with their palms facing outwards. Invite two or three people to say prayers of praise.

Next, invite the group to bring their arms down to their sides, with their hands out, palms facing the ceiling as if receiving a gift. In a few moments of silence, encourage everyone to reflect on their own situation and to meditate on God. If appropriate, individuals may like to use the opportunity to repent and ask for the Holy Spirit to be present in power.

Finally, ask the group to turn round so they are all facing outwards, lifting one hand outstretched to 'the world'. Ask them to think of a mission partner they know or support; or a country close to their hearts. Everybody prays out loud together for their world concern.

Prayer activity 3

Prayer for the Body of Christ

You will need: a wooden cross. If you don't have one available, a cross made from card that could be stuck to the wall would be fine.

Inform the group that this time of prayer will be in different stages. At each stage they are invited to share any thoughts they believe are from God or offer a short prayer that everyone can join in. Ask the group to sit or kneel and close their eyes to begin.

Start by reading Philippians 2:9–11: *Therefore God exalted him to the highest place and gave him the name that is above every name, that at the name of Jesus every knee should bow, in heaven and on earth and under the earth, and every tongue confess that Jesus Christ is Lord, to the glory of God the Father.*

Encourage the group to say short prayers of praise to Jesus. This would also be a good time to humble ourselves before God, asking his forgiveness and confessing Jesus Christ as Lord.

Read 1 Timothy 2:8: *I want men everywhere to lift up holy hands in prayer, without anger or disputing.*

Invite the group to lift their hands in prayer. Pray for God to be at work in the Church and the world. Pray for unity and purpose among Christians.

Read Ephesians 6:13–15: *Therefore put on the full armour of God, so that when the day of evil comes, you may be able to stand your ground, and after you have done everything, to stand. Stand firm then … with your feet fitted with the readiness that comes from the gospel of peace.*

Ask the whole group to stand. Spend time praying that God will empower us by his Spirit to stand firm and have the boldness to spread the message of the gospel of peace.

During this time, quietly place the wooden cross in a central place so that it will be visible when the group open their eyes.

Read Hebrews 12:2: *Let us fix our eyes on Jesus, the author and perfecter of our faith, who for the joy set before him endured the cross, scorning its shame, and sat down at the right hand of the throne of God.*

Ask the group to open their eyes to look at the cross. Spend time thanking God for Jesus.

Prayer activity 4

Travel and pray

You will need: news items and prayer requests written or typed onto small slips of paper (about 10 per continent) researched from newspapers or the Internet. The BBC news website is helpful for research as it has headlines listed by continent.

This activity works well during a church service. Like many of the activities in this book it does require quite a bit of preparation – but it's worth it! The aim is for everyone to be involved in praying for all continents of the world in an intelligent manner.

Choose five areas of your church hall or other space to be prayer stations, each one representing a different part of the world – Africa, the Middle East, Australasia, Europe and the Americas. Ask a different member of the congregation to represent each of the five continents. During the service, these people will stand by their stations and distribute the slips of paper to the congregation near them. If possible, choose people who are from, or have experience of working in, those parts of the world. Perhaps they could dress up in costume from that area, or produce decorations or posters to create a sense of authenticity. The idea is to create the impression for the congregation that they are travelling around the world as they pray.

Open the time of prayer with a reading of Colossians 1:3–9. Now encourage the congregation to move around the continent stations and spend time praying for each part of the world, using the supplied information and prayer requests, but also drawing on any of their own knowledge or contacts.

Prayer activity 5

Flags

You will need: paper; coloured felt-tip pens; an enlarged photocopy of the flag on page 73, coloured if possible.

Flags provide an immediately accessible, colourful and creative way to learn about the world. The aim of this activity – which can be used in church, youth group or small group – is to draw people's attention to a country through the colours of its flag. Sometimes the meaning of a nation's flag is a helpful way to learn new details about that part of the world. The example of Kenya is given below, but you can choose any country of interest to you, your group or church. Spend some time at the end praying for the country you choose.

In advance you will need to research and prepare a presentation about a flag, and also about the country's current needs. A good place to start is Flags of the World: www.fotw.net

There is also a free downloadable Internet game about flags and countries at www.wartoft.nu/software/seterra/

Start by inviting the group to design a flag for themselves. The shapes, symbols and colours need to represent some aspects of their personality, faith, interests or work. Set a time limit. When everyone has finished, show them the Kenyan flag and ask these questions:

1   Do you know where this flag is from?

2   What can you see in the flag?

3   What do the colours of the flag represent?

Describe the colours if you haven't been able to colour the photocopy. The flag consists of three horizontal strips coloured (from top to bottom) black, red and green, separated by narrow white strips. Centrally is a symmetrical Masai shield and spears in white, black and red. The black represents the people of Kenya – 35 million of them, half of whom are under the age of 16. The red represents the blood shed in the country's struggle for freedom; the flag was introduced in 1963 when Kenya gained independence from the British. Green represents the land, rich with natural resources; Kenya has some of the most staggering natural beauty in the world. The white strips signify peace. The shield and spears represent the defence of freedom.

Further ideas for using flags:

If you are involved in leading an all-age service, you could provide flags for the smaller children to colour at the front while you explain the meanings of the colours of the flag to everybody else. Or, with a bit of preparation, small flags photocopied about A6 size could be given to the congregation to take away; the task could be for everyone to find out details about the country whose flag they have been given and pray for it that week.

Prayer activity 6

Pictures in the news

You will need: current newspapers or a computer displaying a news site for the day.

We see so many images from around the world in newspapers and on TV news broadcasts but we rarely stop to ponder the individuals involved in each situation. This short activity is a useful icebreaker for a small group which will hopefully help them look at news images more critically. Not everything is always as it seems! This is also an encouragement to identify with Christians from other nations going through difficult times.

Focus on the news stories that feature people. Invite the group to think about a number of stories, asking the questions below. If it's helpful, give out photocopies of the questions and divide into twos or threes to consider different stories and feed back in turn. Remind everyone that this is not a test – it doesn't matter if they don't complete all the questions; the questions are there to stimulate debate.

Discussion questions:

1   Who is in the picture? What are they doing? What expressions do they have on their faces?

2   Who is not in the picture? Are we being given only one view of the situation?

3   What are your feelings toward the situation, or to the people in the picture?

4   What do you think a Christian would/should do in this situation?

After each report back, have a time of prayer with one or two people praying for the situation in the picture. Pray for any Christians who you imagine may be involved, that they will be given wisdom to know how to be a witness to Jesus in that place.

A HOUSE OF PRAYER FOR ALL NATIONS

And foreigners who bind themselves to the LORD
     to serve him,
to love the name of the LORD
     and to worship him,
all who keep the Sabbath without desecrating it
     and who hold fast to my covenant –
these I will bring to my holy mountain
     and give them joy in my house of prayer.
Their burnt offerings and sacrifices
     will be accepted on my altar;
for my house will be called
     a house of prayer for all nations.

The Lord, speaking in Isaiah 56:6,7

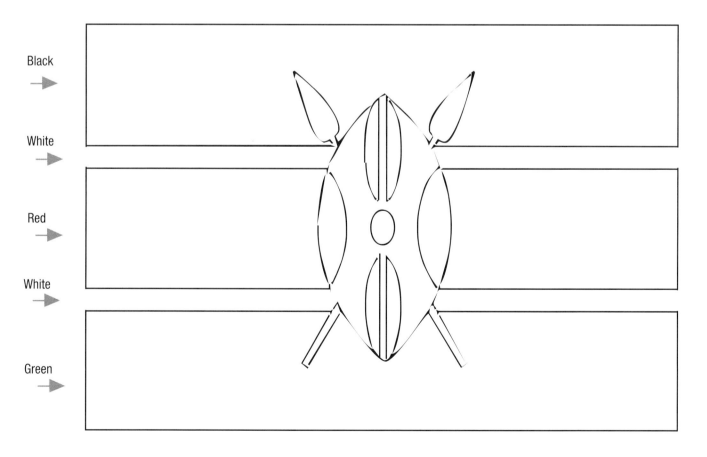

Black →
White →
Red →
White →
Green →

At the centre is a red shield with black ovals on the right and left, half white oval
at the top and bottom, a white oval in the centre, and white spears crossed behind it.

Sketch

Confusing commission

Cast (7 voices)

Pierre de Brush (PdB) – a painter with a French accent
Secretary at the king's palace (Sec)
PA to the king (PAK)
King's publicity guru (KPG) – fast-talking
The queen (Que) – posh accent
Accounts recorded message
Accounts clerk (Acc) – sarcastic tone

Props (optional)

- Telephones (or mobile phones) for each character
- A selection of character-appropriate hats, such as a beret for Pierre de Brush and a crown for the queen
- A label for each character indicating name and job title

Script

PdB *(dials phone)*

Sec *(picks up)*   Hello… the king's palace.

PdB   The palace? Great! I was wondering if I could speak to somebody about a painting I have been commissioned to do for the king.

Sec   Certainly. What name is it, please?

PdB   Pierre de Brush.

Sec   And what painting is it concerning?

PdB   I have the details here in a letter I received from the king (*PdB takes out commission from envelope to read over the phone*). To: Pierre de Brush. Your commission: paint a life portrait of the king in time for his birthday next month. Your commission fee: £10,000.

Sec   Oh, I see… a commission to paint a portrait of the king for his birthday?

PdB   Yes, that's right.

Sec   One moment, please.

PAK   Hello, this is the PA to the king. How can I help you, Mr de Brush?

PdB   Monsieur de Brush.

PAK   Monsieur de Brush, right. Go ahead.

PdB   I have a few questions about this painting I have to do for the king's birthday.

PAK   A portrait, wasn't it?

PdB   That's right. I was wondering if I could arrange a time when the king would sit for me…

PAK	Sit for you?
PdB	Yes, you know… it's to be a life portrait so I'm sure his majesty wanted me to come to the palace, perhaps to paint him sitting on his throne or standing in the royal gardens.
PAK	I'm not sure about that. His majesty is very busy. I'll just check his diary… (*pause*). No, I'm sorry. The king is completely booked up until his birthday.
PdB	Booked up? But how am I supposed to paint him… ?
PAK	Yes, tricky one that. I'll tell you what. I'll pop some pictures in the mail… a few postcards… magazine cuttings… That should give you an impression of what he looks like.
PdB	(*uncertain*) Are you sure?
PAK	Positive! I'm sure you'll do a great job.
PdB	Yes, but are you sure he won't…
PAK	Listen, Mister de Brush. I have another call coming in. I'm going to pass you through to the king's publicity guru. He can answer any more questions you might have.

KPG	Hello. Who am I speaking to?
PdB	Pierre de Brush.
KPG	Hello, Mr de Flush.
PdB	It's de Brush.
KPG	What can I do for you?
PdB	Well, I'm painting the king for his birthday…
KPG	Well, we want a summery, breezy look, lots of light, wind blowing in his majesty's hair, that sort of thing. After the incident with the duck and the underpants the king wants a safe and friendly image in all his publicity and that includes his paintings. Safe and friendly, all right? Anything else?
PdB	(*frantically tries to write some of these things down on his commission paper*) Should he be standing or sitting?
KPG	Neither. He should be playing tennis, I'd say. Make it sporty and athletic. Sporty and athletic, got that?
PdB	(*writing it down*) Playing tennis. Sporty. A – T – H – L…
KPG	Have to go. But the queen would like a word with you.
PdB	What?

Que	Hello, Monsieur de Brush.
PdB	Yes, who's this?
Que	Why, it's the queen.
PdB	Your majesty!
Que	So, Monsieur de Brush, I believe you have been commissioned to make a work of art out of my husband.

PdB	That's correct, your majesty. I have a commission here to paint the king in time for his birthday.
Que	Very good. Now, I should tell you, there's been a slight change of plan.
PdB	(*nervously*) Oh, really. What's that?
Que	You're no longer to paint the king. You're to paint me, that is to say, your commission is to paint the queen.
PdB	(*silence, mouth open*)
Que	Monsieur de Brush?
PdB	I'm sorry, your majesty. It says here…
Que	Be that as it may, these things change. You know how it is, I'm sure. It has been decided that you shall be painting me instead. Could you come in next Tuesday morning?
PdB	Umm… I suppose that should be fine, your majesty. (*frantically crosses out details on his commission, and writes correction*) Not king… paint queen, next… Tuesday…
Que	Very well. I look forward to meeting you, Monsieur de Brush. It has been a pleasure talking with you. Cheerio.

Sec	Hello!
PdB	Hello? Who's this?
Sec	Hello? Who are you?
PdB	I'm Pierre de Brush. Who are you?
Sec	You're through to the king's palace.
PdB	Yes, I know that…
Sec	Oh, hello again, they must have put you through to me again. It's the secretary. Is there anybody you would like to speak to, Monsieur de Brush?
PdB	Umm, let's see (*scratches head and looks forlornly at the commission*). The accounts department?
Sec	One moment, please.

Recorded message

You are through to the palace accounts department. Press 1 if you owe his majesty taxes. Press 2 if you are facing imprisonment for unpaid taxes. Press 3 if you have been commissioned by his majesty to render a service…

PdB	(*pressing his phone keypad*) That's probably it. Three.

Acc	Accounts.
PdB	Yes, I have a query about a commission. I have to paint a picture of the king… well, actually of the queen.
Acc	So, who's it to be? The king or the queen?

PdB	The queen… I think.
Acc	Fine, so you're painting the queen. What's the query?
PdB	Well, it says here (*reading*): Your commission fee is £10,000. I was just wondering,.. will that be by cash or by cheque?
Acc	(*blows a raspberry*) £10,000, yeah right! One moment please… (*brief pause*). I'm sorry, what name was it?
PdB	Pierre de Brush.
Acc	(*after some moments*) I'm sorry, Mr Pierre. There's been a mistake. The king never commissions paintings for this amount. I think somebody typed too many zeros on your commission and put the decimal point in the wrong place. It should read £10. £10 is your commission fee.
PdB	(*stunned*) Excuse moi?
Acc	Your £10 will be paid to you in cash, probably in the form of one crisp unfolded bank note.
PdB	But it clearly says here… (*Pierre reads again*). Your commission fee is £10,000.
Acc	As I say, I think that should read £10.
PdB	(*stammering in bewilderment*) Ten pounds!
Acc	One moment please, Mr Pierre. The PA to the king would like a word.
PAK	Hello there, Mister de Brush?
PdB	(*barely masking his anger*) It's Monsieur…
PAK	Monsieur de Brush. I've just had a brief chat with his majesty. There has been a mistake. In fact, it's supposed to be of the prince. And, it's not supposed to be a painting, it's going to be a sculpture. And it's not for the king's birthday either, it needs to be ready by Christmas. Will that be OK, Mister de Brush? Mister de Brush?

(*PdB has already hung up and is ripping up the commission*)

Other books in the Multi-Sensory series

✳ fresh ✳ innovative ✳ imaginative ✳ inspirational ✳ practical

MULTI-SENSORY CHURCH

Over 30 ready-to-use ideas for creative churches and small groups

Sue Wallace

MULTI-SENSORY PRAYER

Over 60 ready-to-use ideas for creative churches and small groups

Sue Wallace

MULTI-SENSORY SCRIPTURE

50 innovative ideas for exploring the Bible in churches and small groups

Sue Wallace

MULTI-SENSORY TOGETHER

15 ready-to-use sessions for Bible exploration in creative small groups

Ian Birkinshaw

MULTI-SENSORY SEASONS

15 ready-to-use Bible-based sessions through the seasons for creative small groups

Wendy Rayner and Annie Slade

MULTI-SENSORY PARABLES

15 ready-to-use sessions on the stories Jesus told – for creative churches and small groups

Ian Birkinshaw

MULTI-SENSORY PROPHETS

15 ready-to-use sessions on God's messengers – for creative churches and small groups

Mike Law

This series is just part of a wide range of resources for churches and small groups published by Scripture Union.

SU publications are available from Christian bookshops, on the Internet or via mail order. You can:

- phone SU's mail order line: 0845 0706006
- email info@scriptureunion.org.uk
- log on to www.scriptureunion.org.uk
- write to SU Mail Order, PO Box 5148, Milton Keynes MLO, MK2 2YX

wise traveller

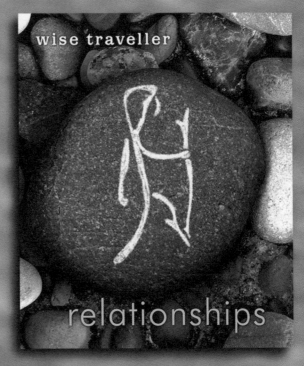

Why doesn't happiness last?
How do I live with loss?
How can I make the most of my relationships?

The *Wise Traveller* series offers meditations for life's journey to people who recognise that life is not neat or painless, but know that it is instead stuffed full of meaning, mystery, beauty and sacred encounters:

- Original reflections, poems and stories, and Christian writings from across history, offer pathways for those seeking a more authentic way of living.

- A creative and open-ended approach to biblical spirituality and prayer.

- An ideal gift for your spiritually open friend, relative, neighbour or colleague.

- Original reflections by *Multi-Sensory* writer Sue Wallace and others known for their experimental approach to Christian spirituality including Steve Hollinghurst, Martin Wroe and Kester Brewin.

£2.99 each